The Money Trap

The Money Trap

A Practical Program to Stop
Self-Defeating Financial Habits
So You Can Reclaim Your
Grip on Life

Ron Gallen

HarperResource
An Imprint of HarperCollins*Publishers*

This book is designed to provide readers with a general overview of personal financial strategies. It is not designed to be a definitive guide or to take the place of advice from a qualified financial planner or other professionals. The author and the publisher expressly disclaim liability from any damage that may result from the use of the information in this book.

HarperCollins books may be purchased for educational, business, or sales promotional use. For information please write: Special Markets Department, HarperCollins Publishers Inc., 10 East 53rd Street, New York, NY 10022.

FIRST EDITION

Designed by Joy O'Meara

Printed on acid-free paper

Library of Congress Cataloging-in-Publication Data

Gallen, Ron.
    The money trap / a practical program to stop self-defeating financial habits so you can reclaim your grip on life.
        p. cm.
    Includes index.
    ISBN 0-06-621158-1
    1. Money—Psychological aspects.   I. Title.

HG222.3 .G35 2002
332.4'01'9—dc21

2001024914

02 03 04 05 06 RRD 10 9 8 7 6 5 4 3 2 1

For Elizabeth

Contents

Contents

Acknowledgments

This book would not have been possible without the guidance, support, and undying encouragement of Kennedy Fraser, Suzanna Lessard, and Susan Cheever, my early readers and patient friends. I am grateful to those special people who kept me going during the times when I doubted myself most: Michael Gallen, Ken Bichel, Jerry Mundis, Mary Carlson, David Wells, Stephanie Laidman, Liz Perle, Judy Collins, Kathy Rich, and Michele Romero. Summertime thanks to Joanna Coles and Peter Godwin—who were there for the beach walks when I just needed them to listen. And to Willow, the world's sweetest dog, with her cutest chocolate poodle nose at my keyboard, nudging me forward.

My ability to write this book at all was due in no small part to the kind and inspired attention of Tony Bass, Ph.D. Thank you for everything, Tony.

How do you thank a group of people who have transformed your life utterly? What do you say to those who you have been charged with helping, but who have delivered you from yourself? To all of you brave souls: Godspeed in your recovery and thank you.

My heartfelt thank you to William Clark, agent extraordinaire.

Special thanks to Megan Newman, my editor at HarperCollins. Her enthusiasm and support, her insight and perspective have been invaluable. Last, to Elizabeth Fagan: who kept the faith and provided the best (often late night) in-house editing anyone could want.

Preface

I have written this book to try to capture the spirit of recovery from money disorders, and to set down the practical solutions I have found for stopping chronic problems with money, work, and debt. For the past eleven years or so, I have been lucky enough to work with hundreds of brave souls who have decided to take control of their lives, to stop their self-defeating patterns with money, and to begin their recovery. My job has been to help them end their compulsive spending, debting, or shopping and to short-circuit their underearning or workaholism. Then, to use a group of simple tools for establishing a more stable and authentic life—one that uses their truest gifts and is full of their deepest desires and dreams.

It's not easy. The nature of a long-standing problem with money, regardless of how many new disguises it may adopt, is that it probably has underlying emotional causes. In that sense, money disorders are not much different from any other compulsive or addictive disorder—treating the symptoms alone doesn't work. For that matter, neither does treating only the underlying dynamics. That's why traditional approaches have so often failed. The advice of lawyers and bankers, accountants and investment advisers doesn't help if you can't stick with it. Bankruptcy or credit and debt counseling doesn't seem to offer a lasting solution either—both act more like a Band-Aid until the inevitable return of the same old problem. Neither has it been my experience that psychotherapy alone usually breaks the compulsive cycle for people stuck in the grip of a money disorder. Money disorders require specialized help: an integrated approach that helps interrupt the self-destructive cycle while reestablishing a supportable financial structure and personal well-being.

My main hope is that this book can do for you what the process I describe here has done for my clients. Many clinicians and helping professionals have asked me over the years to set down the complete process of recovery for them to refer to in helping others. I have tried to do that along with offering the individual sufferer a comprehensive plan for recovery.

All the stories and anecdotes in this book are true. Only the names and some of the identifying details have been changed to protect individual privacy. I hope you might identify with them and with the way they felt more than the exact details of their story. I know I have. My work having grown out of my own terrible money disorder, I have had that powerful feeling wash over me so many times: "Me, too," I have said. "I felt that way, too."

The Money Trap

Introduction

Do you feel out of control with money? Are you in trouble with debt? Constantly worrying about money, or stuck in a pattern of earning less than you deserve? Do you work longer and more intensely than you should? Or have you fallen into an obsession with money, savings, investments, or retirement? If you have, you are not alone. There is an epidemic of money disorders—of feeling bad about ourselves, and our relationship with money.

Even during our recent economic expansion—the longest in history—more people wound up struggling with money and debt than ever before. Since our national focus on money went into hyperdrive, the number of people whose relationship with money is out of control has followed right behind. It may be hard to say which there are more of now, people struggling with their weight or people struggling with their money—it's a pretty close race.

There has never been a shortage of advice about money. The advice people get once they're stuck in a self-defeating cycle with money often goes something like: "The answer is simple. You just need to earn a little more and spend a little less." No kidding! That's like telling compulsive overeaters that all they need to do is eat a little less and exercise a little more. They just can't do it. Breaking a compulsive pattern is hard, especially when it is complicated by deeper needs. It takes willingness and support. And it takes practical actions designed to break the self-destructive cycle.

I have written this book for everyone who is stuck in a self-defeating cycle with money, work, or debt. The point of the book is to assure you that you are not alone. And to give you everything you need to begin the process of healing.

Money Disorders. That's what I call the emotional and spiritual imbalances that express themselves as continuing problems with money and work. The *problem* is not money; it's only the *symptoms* that are about money. The underlying causes of the symptoms run deeper, more to the emotional and spiritual realm. That's why fixes that only address the money problems never work. It is similar to treating someone with appendicitis only for their pain. Morphine will take care of the pain, but without surgery for the underlying condition, the patient usually dies.

There are four main types of money disorder: Overspending, Workaholism, Money Obsession, and Underearning. Overspenders—compulsive spenders, shoppers, and debtors—are pretty easy to recognize. They have at some point lost their ability to control their spending, shopping, or borrowing, and the result is that their lives feel empty, meaningless, or desperate—even hopeless.

Workaholism is a little different. Most workaholics have a hard time seeing that anything is actually wrong; quite the contrary, they wear workaholism as a sort of badge of honor. Workaholism isn't frowned on in our culture—it's encouraged. Workaholism is at such an all-time high that the word has lost most of its original meaning: someone whose addiction to work meant that they foreclosed on aspects of their larger life—such as sustaining intimate relationships, nourishing their creativity, or tending to spiritual development.

Money Obsession—or being obsessed with money, savings, investments, or retirement—is certainly not new. What is new, however, is the giant increase in how many people have fallen into this obsession, and its stark intensity.

Then there is Underearning. Underearners are those who can't seem to regularly earn enough to take care of their needs, don't get paid as much as might be expected given their education, talents, and training, and have difficulty advocating on their own behalf. This category also includes those who become hoarders, or anorectic spenders, in fear of there never being enough. Understanding the phenomenon of the underearner is somewhat newer, more out of view. The essence of an underearning problem is keeping yourself under wraps; it's about lacking the power to embrace yourself truly and to risk bringing yourself out into what feels like a scary, competitive world.

We all have a powerful relationship with money. We instill it with all sorts of powers—some of which it has, most of which it doesn't. The idea that money can solve your problems may not be true, but it can be a pretty persistent illusion. We can go a long way toward explaining money disorders when we understand that we expect a whole lot more from money than it will ever be able to deliver. We use our intense focus on it to protect against unwanted feelings; we hope it will fill the void in our hearts and in our souls. We fantasize that if we can just get our hands on enough of the stuff, all our troubles will disappear.

Since what we seek in money is not what is really missing, what we find in money is never enough. No matter how much we find. When we ask money to do for us what it cannot do, we set up a self-perpetuating cycle that leads to despair. We lose control of our spending and debts pile up or, in the case of the underearner, we purposely stay small to avoid the scary world out there. Or we use the intensity of our work to avoid our feelings.

For the past eleven years I have helped hundreds of people suffering with money disorders to establish a supportable financial structure and to live an abundant life. They've made the switch away from having money be the focus of their lives, to money helping them live their lives. Of course, everyone proceeds at their own pace. I've worked with people who just needed a tune-up, and they were soon back on track. And I've worked with some whose resistance to change is formidable, and whose progress is more halting. I haven't met anyone yet whose money disorder couldn't be healed, given a willingness to follow a simple plan for recovery. Here it is again: no matter how impossible your situation feels to you now, if you follow this simple process, you will be able to recover. I'm not saying it's easy; I'm saying recovery is there for you if you are willing.

Ultimately, the challenge is to break the old pattern, to adopt a plan for taking care of ourselves in a wholly new way. The result is a way out of fear, and into a life of fulfilling our hopes, dreams, and desires.

The Impossible Dream

We are a nation preoccupied with money. Sometimes it seems as if there is an apparatus, powered by our national psyche, that is super-saturating the air with money molecules. Every schoolboy knows how much his classmate's sneakers cost. No one dreams of growing up to be president anymore. It's all about making the big score now. Money has become the central way we view ourselves, and how we measure our self-esteem. The idea that money is the answer, no matter what the question, has hijacked our collective soul. Envy has become our new national *zeitgeist*. And they say that envy is the one deadly sin that actually brings no pleasure.

The intense focus we put on money, the tantalizing stories of big scores and easy money, and the general atmosphere of envy they evoke, has left many of us in trouble with money and debt. To give you an idea of the magnitude of the problem, there have been 4 million personal bankruptcies in just the past three years. That is a new all-time record, and it's a new record by a mile. That means there was one bankruptcy for every thirty American households in only the past three years. To put it in historical perspective—bankruptcies increased by 600 percent during the eighties and nineties, prompting Congress to vote for tough new provisions in their overhaul of existing bankruptcy laws that seem likely to take effect soon.

And those who go bankrupt are just the critical, visible part of the problem. We love the stories about IPO millionaires and billionaires who talk about how their dream came true after they maxed out their credit cards to get started. But for every IPO millionaire, there are thousands who just get into deeper and deeper trouble with debt. The fact is that most people who max out their credit cards, for any reason, wind up with just that: maxed-out cards.

Last year, 3 *billion* solicitations for credit cards were sent out in the United States. That is eleven pieces of mail inviting you to get a new credit card for every man, woman, and child in the country. This despite a record number of people unable to make the payments on their current cards.

Owing to their near ubiquity, it is hard to believe that general-use credit cards have been around for only about thirty years. Along with their ascension, however, has come an explosion of people in trouble with debt. Coupled with the heady atmosphere of the booming economy and the envy it has evoked, the easy get-it-now-pay-for-it-later ethos has backfired on millions. Many have found themselves in the grip of something they had no idea they might lose control of.

Total credit card debt has become a runaway train that doubled in this country in the six years between 1988 and 1994. Then it *doubled again* between 1994 and 1999. In the past year, it has gone up from $560 billion to $650 billion. That means that the 60 million households who carry balances have an average total credit card debt of $11,000. Unmanageable debt has become such a widespread problem for so many people that the entire second mortgage industry has been recast and remarketed as "debt consolidators." You can hardly escape the marketing blitz of selling home equity loans as "debt consolidation" solutions. Who doesn't know the catchphrase: "When your bank says No, Champion says Yes."

You may not be surprised to hear, then, that home equity debt has doubled in the past six years. Over 5,000 households *per day* use equity loans to pay off their credit card debt. Recently, the total amount of home equity debt outstanding in the country became equal to the amount of credit card debt outstanding. In other words, a wholesale move has taken place toward paying off unmanageable credit card debt with home equity debt.

And that can be a big problem. Most people who take out a home equity loan to pay off their credit card debt swear they'll never get into that bind again. They reason that since they now have a longer-term loan to pay off, they have lower monthly payments they can afford—that they dodged the proverbial bullet. So they heave a sigh of relief. Whew!

But swear as they may that they will not get into debt trouble again, that is precisely what happens. According to a recent study, only 30 percent of home equity borrowers had no new credit card debt just eleven months after the loan closed. On average, they had run up another $2,200 in credit card debt on top of their "debt consolidation loan."

I can tell you that I see a lot of these people a year or two down the road and they have as much credit card debt as ever, very often more. Only now they have the home equity loan and payments, too. So their problem hasn't been solved, it's been doubled. Put off a couple of years, but doubled nonetheless.

Debt can become unmanageable quickly. It is never very hard to justify using that credit card one more time—no matter how much you owe. Alongside home equity debt consolidation, there has been an extraordinary increase in debt counseling centers in the past years as well. Only a few short years ago no one had even heard of credit counseling agencies, such as Budget and Credit Counseling or Consumer Credit Counseling; now there are more than 2,000 of these agencies. They're everywhere. I saw a billboard for a consumer credit counseling service when I was in South Florida recently. Right there on I-95, between Miami and Fort Lauderdale, as big as you please, was a picture of a life preserver, and at the top it read: DROWNING IN DEBT? while across the bottom it cried, "CALL 1-800-SAVE-ME-TOO."

If there have been 4 million bankruptcies in the past three years, there are probably just as many people going to credit counseling agencies. And it certainly seems like a good idea to offer counseling to those who find themselves in chronic trouble with debt. But what they really offer on closer inspection is a Band-Aid-type fix, the morphine for appendicitis. These credit counseling agencies do the same thing as the home equity people: arrange longer terms and lower payments, with the added caveat that you have to rip up your credit cards. That's a good idea as far as it goes. The problem is that it doesn't go very far.

The Addictive Nature of Money Disorders

Take the example of a person arrested for driving while intoxicated. I think we can probably agree that not everyone who gets arrested for that reason is an alcoholic. But the statistics for those who get arrested again and again for driving while intoxicated are instructive indeed: it is estimated that 25 percent of those arrested for their first DWI are alcoholics; the percentage climbs to near 70 percent for those arrested for their second DWI; and just about everyone who has three or more DWI arrests can be classified as an alcoholic.

Are those numbers a big surprise? Probably not, precisely because those who are not alcoholic are able to control themselves after that first arrest—the threat of increasing consequences is enough to deter them from sitting behind the wheel again after they have been drinking. Certainly if they are foolish enough to try it again and get arrested a second time, the trouble they get into with the law is more than enough to warn them off drinking and driving. But alcoholics don't respond that way. Their craving for a drink, and how they think after they begin drinking are different from that of the nonalcoholic.

The same is true for people in chronic trouble with money and debt. They are in the grip of something far deeper than simple imprudence. The trouble created by not being able to support their expenses doesn't give them an early warning, nor do collection threats serve as much of a deterrent. They go by deeper needs; they go by craving and a marked powerlessness in their credit card use, and in their inability to accept the limitations of their financial situation. They are like the alcoholic who keeps driving drunk—they need help to stop.

Compulsive and self-defeating problems with money and work are the fastest-growing addictive problem in our country.

If there are 8 million or so people in bankruptcy and credit counseling, there are countless millions who are still spinning the plates in the air, knowing that their fate is inevitably to come crashing down around them. You don't have to come to the point of bankruptcy or debt counseling to begin to feel the heat. Once the compulsive cycle of spending and debt begins, you get rumblings fairly early on that this will not end well. And it doesn't take long to realize that even though your creditors may not be knocking at your door yet, you are heading in that direction, and the brakes seem to have stopped working.

Debt and the College Campus

A disturbing recent development is how many younger people are getting into trouble. Debt tends to start in college these days. Leaving aside the huge problem of students carrying burdensome student loan loads, a recent poll showed that 81 percent of students had their first credit card by the end of their freshman year. The average balance carried by college students was $2,000. But that figure doesn't reveal the more disturbing aspect—that problems controlling credit card use are plaguing large numbers of college students. A new lexicon has even developed on campuses: Visa and MasterCard are commonly referred to as "Monopoly money" or "Yuppie food stamps." Twenty percent of students carry card balances over $10,000.

I don't know how widespread the extreme cases on campus have become, but CNN recently reported two cases in which college kids committed suicide, leaving behind notes saying that their crushing debts were the reason.

They say that money can't buy happiness, and it can't. But there's one problem—we don't believe it. The great fantasy is that when we get a certain amount of money, or can even pretend that we have it, it will be the answer to all our dreams. But money doesn't have that power. The truth is that money can do only two things: buy goods and buy services. Oh, it does those two things very well indeed—it just doesn't do the other stuff.

Simply stated, money cannot buy what money cannot buy. Logically we know that; emotionally we don't. Money is the ultimate example of that most futile of endeavors: using an external source to fill internal needs.

Money substitutes in the external world for feelings in the internal world. And it is never easy to figure out what part of our response comes purely from today, and what part comes from some long-ago emotional realm. You think you're arguing with your wife about how much she spent on that blouse, but you realize your anger has gone far beyond the blouse. The other woman in the office gets the promotion you were hoping for and you feel bad, but that doesn't explain why you couldn't stop how bad you felt about yourself afterward. Money carries a heavy load of emotional freight and family history. Our ideas about money don't get formed in adulthood. They go way back when, and they go way down deep. We may think we really need that new car or that new house—but maybe what we are still trying to do, after all these years, is prove ourselves worthy to a withholding father or a disapproving mother. I'm not saying this is a conscious process. But money does a better job of being two things at one time than anything I know.

Using money and spending to fill inner needs can be viewed, then, as an emotional or spiritual effort at self-healing. It is a misguided effort, but a genuine one nonetheless. I'm sure you can guess what happens when we try to fill inner needs with outer resources—it doesn't work out very well. The problem is that even when all the evidence proves that your way isn't working, you still keep at it for as long as you can, because some part of you is *convinced* that this is the answer.

Once money and debt are out of control in your life, you would think that somehow you would stop, regroup, and initiate some changes that would break the self-destructive pattern. That is nothing like what usually happens: What happens is you do the same old things expecting different results—perhaps you even step up the pace a bit. These patterns with money die hard because on some powerful emotional level, we do not want to face the alternatives. Most people who fall into an obsessive cycle with money and debt don't break the cycle until they have run out of options. Because the things they spend money on don't fill them up, they keep spending more and more in an effort to feel better.

It's about Self-Care

Recovering from a money disorder means learning to take care of yourself. It doesn't matter how selfish or indulgent you may look to those around you, if you have a money disorder, you are really depriving yourself. Breaking a compulsive money cycle means developing a way to take care of yourself in every respect.

I believe that money disorders are a way to avoid feeling all our intense feelings. If you have a money disorder, it is probably a safe bet that you also have deep wells of fear, anger, and sadness that have remained off-limits. The idea of approaching them unprotected is so scary that a money disorder might actually be seen most simply as a misdirection, the way a magician directs your attention to what seems like the real action, while he plies his trick out of plain view. Money says, "Look over here. It's all about the money." After all, that's a whole lot easier than having a look at whatever the deeper needs really are.

Money disorders interrupt your natural ability to live according to your own authentic values. The longing for money or power substitutes for the authentic longings. When we live for money, we neglect our heart.

I believe that money disorders are, at their core, a block to our natural energy and our natural freedom. They ultimately leave us unable to freely give love, and to receive love.

It's not easy. But those who have accepted their problem, and have stuck with the actions outlined in the recovery program, cannot imagine why they waited so long.

Money Disorders

There are probably as many unique money disorders as there are people who struggle with them. But for our purposes, people with these disorders break down into four main types: Overspenders, Workaholics, Money Obsessives, and Underearners.

Overspenders are by far the biggest group. And they are the most obvious group; everyone knows someone who is an overspender. They live above their means, get into trouble with debt, and struggle to keep their heads above water when the deluge comes. Primarily, they use money and spending to bind the high level of anxiety they feel, and to give a boost to a flagging sense of self-esteem. Regardless of how confident or even self-indulgent their exteriors, it is likely that money and spending are being used to compensate for how bad—not how good—they feel about themselves.

I think of overspenders as having come to a fork in the psychic road at some point in their lives: they want something, they can't afford it, and they can't tolerate that feeling. What do they do? Simple—they buy the thing anyway, and damn the consequences. That is what binds their anxiety, delivers a temporary feeling of well-being, and thereafter becomes a deep-seated pattern.

After thousands of these not-so-conscious episodes—the inability to hold certain feelings and the temporary relief that spending brings—we can pretty well predict what happens: debts pile up, creditors demand payments, and a general inability to live within their means takes over. To soothe the guilt and the shame they feel, what do they do? Paradoxically, they spend some more. That is what they are programmed to do. The whole thing is doomed to stop working eventually, however; the wolf is just too strong for the door. Ultimately, they find themselves in trouble—juggling payments to stay afloat, dodging creditors, rationalizing behavior they once abhorred—and desperately trying to keep the surface looking as good as possible for as long as possible.

Next is Workaholism. It is so pervasive these days that the very word seems to have taken on a new meaning in our lexicon. Workaholics don't view their addiction to work as a bad thing at all. Quite the contrary; they're proud of how "dedicated" they are. They're proud of how well established their work ethic is. And they think their willingness to sacrifice is somehow noble, or at least that it is the minimum requirement for entering the land of plenty. But their disorder is exactly the same as that of the overspender: work stands in for other connections in life. It is used to fill the void inside.

I think we can rightfully say that workaholism has reached an epidemic level. Neither is it all that easy these days to distinguish between ambition and addiction. When work becomes an obsession, feelings don't get processed. All manner of goals and values and dreams get attached to the work, and the cycle takes on a life of its own. The expectation (or justification) is that the intense focus on work will someday yield the result that will make it all worthwhile: a windfall of money will arrive; you'll make partner, sell the business, be set for life; your kids will be set for life; who-knows-how-many-generations will be set for life. If there is any awareness that the work ethic is an obsession, an addiction, the idea is dismissed or denied.

Foreclosing on emotional, physical, or spiritual needs hardly feels like a sacrifice at first; it doesn't feel that way until much further down the progressive path. Then the sacrifices can begin to feel intolerably real. The idea is debunked that when some certain monetary or work goal is reached, all problems will be solved. That is not what happens. What happens is that when you get there—there is no *there*, there. Work addiction's proximate reason for being is to achieve money or status or power. On the preconscious level its function is to stand in for things that feel too big to contain, such as overwhelming feelings.

Then there is Money Obsession. Money obsession describes any-one who has money at the center of their lives, who are obsessed with it one way or another, but do not fall mainly into another of the main categories. They are just as obsessed with money as any of the others, but they have different primary symptoms. Money obsessives can include people who come from privileged backgrounds and have lost their ambition, as well as those obsessed with investing and trading who can no sooner tear themselves away from their computer screen than an inveterate gambler can tear himself away from the crap game—in short, those whose emotional life is tied up in their rela-tionship with money.

Money obsession can be the main focus of your life—even when it doesn't seem to be. Maybe making money has become the only thing that feels real, so much so that obsessives are steeped in money, but have no idea how central it is to their psychic landscape. I'm reminded of the fish in the water—the wise, old fish comes upon a group of cocky, young fish, hanging out and generally trying to be as cool as they can be. "How's the water, boys?" the old fish asks as he swims away. Looking more than just a little puzzled, they turn to each other. "What the heck is water?"

Money obsessives often have a "magic number" that—it is their fondest belief—will make them set for life, and release them from all the quotidian cares of the world. The main problem is that once the "magic number" is achieved, or the business becomes successful, or the promotion or partnership or professorship or *whatever* is earned— a new and improved goal rushes in to take its place. Either you up the ante and keep playing the game, or you swallow a large chunk of painful truth—that you devoted your life to an illusion.

Last, there is the flip side of the coin: Underearners. If overspenders spend to bind anxiety and go into debt because their spending urges are beyond their control, what underearners do is essentially the opposite. They are responding to the same cues from the world, and they have the same kind of emotional and spiritual longing that attaches itself to money as do overspenders. But their response to those same cues is very different indeed. Underearners try to keep their world small enough to feel safe. They mostly keep their spending small, and they tend to earn less than they deserve, because they are unable to assert themselves in the competitive world. They are afraid that there isn't enough out there, so they better conserve their resources against a cold and unforgiving world. Maybe overspenders outnumber underearners by so much in my experience only because they are eventually forced to do *something* to get out of the jam that their lives inevitably become. Underearners, on the other hand, often live in quiet deprivation indefinitely, or until they are blessed with either the inspiration or the desperation to change.

Underearners come to that same spot that overspenders do: they want something, can't afford it, and can't tolerate the feelings. What do *they* do? Buy it? No way. What underearners do is to shrink their world a little bit so they don't want the thing anymore—thereby avoiding any disappointment at not getting it. And that's what works to bind *their* anxiety, to quell their fears, and that becomes their pattern.

Ultimately, if their fantasies were played out to the logical yet absurd conclusion, they would become invisible or at least have no needs, the world being viewed as too damned scary. The main fear is that there is not enough to go around out there.

Warning Signs

Just about everyone struggles with money at one time or another. But I don't think it is difficult to distinguish between an episodic difficulty with money, and a chronic syndrome or a very recognizable pattern over a long period of time.

Here are some of the signs and danger signals of money disorders:

Preoccupation with money

People might reasonably be expected to be thinking more about money if things are a little tight and the bills are due, or if their children are about to go to college, or if they are due for a raise and are wondering how much it might be. That is very different from being preoccupied with money most of the time, regardless of what is happening.

No time for anything but work

The person who accepts some overtime or who works intensely for a certain period is quite different from someone who can hardly think of anything but work, or can find no time for anything but work.

The fantasy that a certain amount of money will end all problems

Occasionally fantasizing about what would be different if only you were rich stands in stark contrast to being compelled by a permanent fantasy that a certain amount of money will be the answer to all your problems.

Feeling like there's never enough

I once heard someone with a money disorder say the thing that captures this best. When asked what he likes best, he responded simply, "More."

Chronic envy

The corrosive feeling that kills you when others get what you want, what you deserve. And you don't.

Trouble with creditors

Getting an isolated call from a creditor is one thing. Being in trouble with creditors on a regular basis is another. Trouble with creditors on a regular basis is a fairly sure sign of an entrenched money disorder.

Trouble with the IRS

The IRS is one of the favorite ways for a compulsive debtor to borrow, especially if they are self-employed or own their own business. After all, the IRS is the creditor who gives you the *de facto* biggest credit line, with the absolute easiest access—you simply don't pay your taxes, thereby borrowing the money.

Afraid of the mail, afraid of the phone

If creditors become a real problem, eventually fear of the shame cycle their calls induce can lead to being afraid to answer the phone or to open the mail. Similarly, if your world is shut down enough, and you worry that you don't have the wherewithal to somehow pull it together, the phone and the mail can take on the aspect of a disdainful parent who is fully expected to validate your internal view of yourself as not worthy, as a failure.

Inability to earn enough to meet needs

Underearning is a deceptive and subtle thing. One can always argue that the amount of money earned is a function of the job, of the salary level of the industry in general, or determined more by economic factors outside rather than within their control. The further argument that they are doing the best they can, or that they are doing the best they ever have, can seem to suggest that underearning or deprivation is not really the problem. Earning a relatively small salary is not the hallmark of the underearner; rather it is a continuous or chronic way of always finding oneself deprived of the comforts and satisfactions one could reasonably expect.

Able to pay only the minimums (or less) on credit card balances

The truth is pretty clear here. Running up credit card balances until your debt means you can only afford the minimum payments is a sign of a money disorder. The argument might be made that circumstances beyond your control were at work, that anyone would be in the same boat. *But anyone would not be in the same boat.* Those without a money disorder would reduce expenses to avoid going further into debt—no matter what that entailed. And they would be able to do so because they would not shrink from the hard choices if the alternative was being a slave to debt.

Erratic work history

Certainly, no particular work history is diagnostic and clearly indicates a money disorder. Erratic work history does, however, plague underearners far more than it does other populations. Somehow their lack of confidence in their abilities, or their suspicion that they will be "found out" works to undermine their success, or even leads to dismissal. A promising business venture is somehow sabotaged by doubt or fear. A new job in a new industry is tried, but all efforts feel doomed from the start, based on nothing more than a thought like: "Why did

I think I could possibly succeed any better here?" On the indulgent side, arrogance and grandiosity do their dirty work, maybe captured as: "I know better than that jerk who they call my boss."

Fear of financial insecurity

Fear of financial insecurity has nothing to do with how much financial security you have. It sounds crazy, but it's true. I know a man with $20 million whose fear of financial insecurity could be described as complete: he pretty much worries about it constantly. I similarly know a woman whose earnings meet only a modest lifestyle but who does work she loves to support herself and her daughter. Her fear of financial insecurity is nearly nonexistent. Fear of financial insecurity is an emotional symptom, not a financial one. Not having financial security is just that—not having financial security. How you feel about it is something else that is not based on money.

Work doesn't seem to fit with talents or goals

Curious lapses of judgment are another hallmark of money disorders. When it has to do with your own well-being, otherwise sound reasoning and decision making processes fail. Working at a job that has nothing to do with your individual talents and gifts is so common as to be a cliché. It is also a way to ensure that you will not grow to your full potential. It is one thing to do less than optimal work in order to achieve a specific and short-term goal; it is another when that is a chronic syndrome or life pattern.

Unrealized potential

I see far too many truly gifted people working ridiculously below their potential. It is not that there is no demand for their skills and ingenuity in the marketplace—theirs are internal roadblocks. Fear of failure and fear of success become synonymous. Some don't bother trying because rejection is too intolerable. Sometimes, fear of people or difficulty in certain work environments conspires to keep the lid on.

In any case, a thousand rationales for staying small are readily available, but finding the courage to replace them with the more authentic goal—becoming whatever you are capable of—remains elusive.

Feelings of self-worth inordinately attached to money, power, or position

If your self-esteem depends upon outside sources, life will not feel very safe. When money or power occupy center stage because any sense of well-being depends on them, there is no end to the power-driven lusting for them. Neither money and power nor position actually works at providing self-esteem; and if a round peg doesn't fit a square hole, neither will a million round pegs fit either. The spiral of obsession, therefore, does not usually get broken until an admission that what is being built is an illusion.

Obsessive involvement with investments, savings, and strategies for financial security

This is a fast-growing segment. The advent of the Internet has given rise to a whole new generation of money-obsessed addicts. The easy access to all sorts of information fuels the obsession with amassing a big enough pile of money to insulate you from the troubles of the world. Something like: "If I can only get my hands on $——, then I'll be okay," or "I have to find the mutual funds that will beat the Dow or the S&P in order not to feel like a chump." Planning prudently for retirement is one thing; worrying incessantly about how much will be enough and how to get that much is another. The people I have worked with who have amassed substantial money but have foreclosed on large quadrants of life in the offing report that the sacrifices weren't worth it, and that they had not become the vision of themselves as they were in their fantasies. The obsessive quest exacted a price not payable in money.

So the key to a money disorder is not whether you are experiencing financial difficulties or not. Remember that there is a dramatic difference between a temporary or anomalous problem, and something more like a major life theme.

The next section of the book is devoted to describing each type of money disorder in depth, and to some of the stories that I hope can illuminate them.

But first my own story.

My Story

I grew up in love with money. I think I must have been as young as five years old when I first got the idea that if I only had enough money, everything would be all right. Money was so central to my psychic makeup that if I tried hard enough, I could almost imagine dollar signs attached to the neurotransmitters firing across the synapses in my brain. I was always the kid who had the most successful lemonade stand, and the one who found the best-paying after-school jobs. I was the one the whole family called precocious. I quit college, impatient to make lots of money. And I did earn a lot. But money didn't really deliver; I was always just as afraid when I had money as when I didn't. Maybe more so. What I found is the same thing every seeker who sanctifies money eventually does—I had sought the wrong thing.

I come by this thing honestly. Money was the main theme in my family story. My father's brother was extremely rich; my father was not. Although my father worked for his brother in the same office for more than thirty years, they never spoke. The atmosphere in our house was infused with envy, but we never said a word about it. Feelings about money were intense, but they seemed to float in the ether rather than be set down where we could examine them. And they hovered out there for me while I remained in money's thrall. The only sign that something was wrong was when I had one of my regular psychosomatic symptoms, or had to visit the local emergency room with an anxiety attack that inevitably felt like a heart attack to me.

When we were young, my brother and I loved to play Monopoly. We devised a sophisticated system of credit, which allowed us to build as many hotels as we wanted on any property. If you landed on Boardwalk with ten hotels, you owed $20,000. Since there was not enough cash in the Monopoly bank to pay, we kept ledgers of who owed whom how much, as if we were traders on the floor of a financial exchange. When I was nine years old, I owed my brother 2 million Monopoly dollars.

This idea of getting enough money so that I could feel insulated from the pressures of the world came with the attendant need to spend like crazy. My sense of self-worth was so tenuous that I needed some external way of signifying that I was all right, which is a whole lot easier than actually looking at what might be wrong. So I bought stuff. If anyone were to ask me what I wanted, I always knew the answer—I wanted all the great stuff. I needed to make sure that I always had enough money—or was able to spend as if I had enough money—to keep from feeling terrible about myself (although I certainly never thought in those terms at the time).

I got my first credit card when I was eighteen. I had my first credit card taken away from me when I was nineteen. Even at the height of my earning, I was always flirting with the limits on my cards—and I had lots of cards. In fact, the more I earned, the further in debt I seemed to go. Not always, no. But inevitably. Over any substantial period of time, my entanglements with money always got worse. Sometimes I would catch a glimpse of myself and know that the cycle I was in would not end well, indeed was not going well. I was not spending my life in a way that resonated to any deep place in me, and

I was certainly not expressing my creative soul. I was chained to my need for more of everything, and there wasn't that much air left in the chamber where I lived. But even in those moments of recognition, I would convince myself that my new Mercedes, or the beautiful woman on my arm was all the proof I needed that things were just fine. I never conceived of doing things differently. It was not until life intervened that a pivotal moment took place. I think of it now as a moment full of grace—when my perspective changed and opened up a tie-line between my overactive mind and my underfed heart.

I was thirty-five and burned out. Living on the edge had left me with very little wiggle room when a business setback happened. Creditors were all over me, and I felt deeply ashamed. I tried to keep the plates in the air for a while, but I knew they were destined to come crashing down this time. I sold the East Hampton place and then the Mercedes, I auctioned the antiques, and I moved to a tiny apartment that could have qualified as a light-free zone. During the deluge, the stomachaches I had were so bad that I thought I probably had a tumor, or at least something inoperable that would leave me in intractable pain. I think the pain more or less ebbed and flowed along the lines of the creditor's calls. Collection guys are very good at what they do. No longer buoyed by money, I felt the weight of what I had been keeping at bay, too. I had, as alcoholics say, hit bottom.

My dear friend Frank, who recently passed away, suggested the most profound yet simple advice I had ever heard. Frank said, "I know your situation has made you feel a little hopeless, but don't you know the secret?" (The *secret*—how ever did he know I was always looking for the *secret*?) "The secret," he said, "is this: Begin where you are. Do what you can do. Proceed in faith. And expect God to help." Everything else, he said, was out of my hands. Those words became my guide, and my balm. Never had advice been more apropos. It was from that crucible of fear I was in, and with my friend's words as a sort of spiritual prescription, that I forged my new beginning.

I think I had a tectonic-plate-type shift, a psychic rearrangement.

My defining beliefs no longer defined me. Or at least I knew I didn't want money to be the driving force in my life anymore. If money was my addiction, the answer obviously could not be to abstain. I wasn't cut out for the monastic life, so I didn't stop using money. Quite the contrary. It has been by penetrating the very heart of my relationship with money and realigning my priorities that I have set myself free from my obsession. I changed my relationship with money, and that changed my whole life. I choose life now, not money. Money facilitates the life I want to live, instead of being the obsessive focus of it.

It's been thirteen years since that fateful time, and I've been blessed not only with a wholesale change in my life but with the gift of being able to pass along my experience and message of hope to many others. I remember thinking after some time, and for the first time in my life, "So this is what it feels like to have the wind at your back." Looking back at my path, I see many evolutionary changes in myself—instead of becoming someone I don't recognize, rather I am becoming who I most truly am, without all the defenses I had erected to keep me safe. They didn't work.

T. S. Eliot said you may travel the world around, but your travels will bring you back to the place where you began—only to know it for the first time.

able to him that he can't stop—even in the midst of lawsuits and mar-shals and foreclosure threats.

Most casual observers are at a loss to understand why Billy doesn't just see the logic of his situation and do something about it. But addicts do not go by logic. They go by deeper needs. They go by crav-ing, and by relief seeking. They do whatever works to get them through. And nothing works better to soothe the troubled soul of a compulsive spender or debtor than spending money.

Compulsive debtors like Billy believe that the stuff they buy will insulate them somehow from their deepest doubts and fears. At least they act that way. They would rather keep on keeping on for as long as they possibly can, even when the abyss comes into view, than face reality one minute before they have to. The more they act as if they can afford the way of life that they imagine will deliver them from want, the more the reality of spending beyond their means validates their original fear—that they don't deserve any better.

When your sense of self-worth is entangled with your earnings, with the things you have, and with the impression that gives the world—then your feelings about those things will probably rule the day rather than any sense of planning or prudence. Keeping pace with your own self-regulated image of how you're doing becomes a very demanding job.

Not everyone who gets into trouble with compulsive debt is as extreme as Billy, however. Rebecca, for one, is at a loss to explain why she finds herself in debt. She is a compulsive debtor who can-not understand how she got into so much trouble. She could list for you, chapter and verse, why each of her decisions is really just the nat-ural and right thing to do. Except that when you add them up, she has had to borrow hundreds and often thousands of dollars each month to support her spending.

Rebecca is a freelance musician and music teacher. She regularly earns about $50,000 a year. She regularly spends about $60,000 a year.

Rebecca does not mean to spend more than she earns—she is forever putting herself on budgets. She just doesn't seem able to keep to them. Certain things always turn out to be budget-busters but somehow impossible to resist. She can't understand how she can earn $50,000 and still be in debt. And she is in debt for more than $70,000. She is a single mom with a teenage daughter. She hasn't been on a vacation in three years (something she is quick to note). And she doesn't buy herself expensive clothes (something she is also quick to point out). She seems to imply that someone else has spent the money that she now owes. But no one else spent the money—it just seems that way to Rebecca, because she feels so much like a victim in all of this. She says that dealing with the creditors who are relentlessly calling her, and with the tidal wave of feelings that accompany the calls is the hardest thing she has ever had to do in her life.

When describing how she lives, however, she leaves a few things out. Most compulsive spenders and debtors do. In her case, for instance, when her daughter wants something, she is rarely able to say no, no matter how expensive. Her daughter *does* wear expensive clothes, and does have expensive lessons and trips. For Rebecca's part, she can't resist old and often very expensive musical scores (she justifies these purchases by reminding herself of all the luxuries she doesn't buy). She is also partial to certain collectibles, and to redecorating with unusual fabrics and furnishings. In fact, it is true that she would probably not be in debt without these particular indulgences—the rest of her life is lived in a fairly modest way.

It's not about the money

Everyone chooses his or her own poison. Those who find themselves in a compulsive debting cycle get there in their own unique way and often can't understand why other people get in trouble with money the way *they* do. How much money they earn never seems to matter very much either. Rebecca is always saying that if she only made $100,000 a year she would never have money troubles. That is hardly very likely. Besides, I have heard that sentiment from just about every compulsive debtor I have ever met—the idea that their problem would be solved with some more money. It never is.

Envy is a vicious thing. It is also the animating feeling behind the acquisitive culture we live in. Trying to find your self-worth by comparing yourself to others never leads anywhere good. For one thing, there is never any dearth of examples to make you feel bad about yourself. No matter how much you have, someone has more. For that matter, no matter how little you have, someone has less. Compulsive spenders and debtors usually feel either far superior to people, or totally inferior. They either feel like King of the Hill, or like they should crawl underneath it.

It's about the feelings

Compulsive debtors do not tolerate their intense feelings very well. So they do the next best thing: learn not to have them. The feelings don't go very far, though—they just come out sideways—as anxiety or panic attacks, for example. Compulsive spenders tend to somatize their feelings, to become hypochondriacs. Hypochondriacs worry that some insignificant physical sensation is actually a heart attack, or that a common headache is really a malignant tumor. Bouts of depression are so common as to be inextricable. The thing about compulsive spenders and debtors is that when things get difficult, when they truly need to come to their own aid with comfort and reassurance, that is when they abandon themselves most. Even hate themselves.

Relying on other people's money undermines self-esteem at the most basic level. When you feel as if the money you earn can't support you (and compulsive debtors feel this way no matter how much they earn), the pressure is always on. But the big picture is most often formed with small strokes, in everyday life decisions.

Consider Elizabeth, a freelance architect and single mother of two young children. She has worked her way up to earning the $120,000 a year Rebecca dreams of. Like Rebecca, she is at a loss to understand how she got into the trouble she is in. After all, she says, she earns, "$120,000 a year." Nevertheless, creditors call her day and night. She cannot even come close to making all the minimum payments they are demanding, along with paying all her other bills. And she is often frantically running to a friend to borrow some cash, or to get a cash advance on her card when there is any credit available, to get her through until she gets paid next. The school she sends her daughter to has threatened to kick the child out if the tuition is not brought up to date. Elizabeth now owes $164,000, and that does not include the back taxes she knows she also owes but has not figured out yet because she is too scared.

She does not see how any of her spending has been extravagant or indulgent; nor does she see how she could do things very much differently. She feels as if she has done what any good single mother would do for herself, and for her children. She says her friends certainly spend significantly more than she does. The reason she is so frantic now is that she has finally run out of credit. There is no way left for her to borrow to keep everything going anymore.

Elizabeth sends both her children to private school in Manhattan. The tuition totals $1,950 a month, and Elizabeth says that it is her highest priority, that she is ready to sacrifice in most other areas to continue to afford it. But the other areas don't come in for much compromise when it is decision time. The rent on her Manhattan apartment is $4,200 a month. She eats out with friends three or four times a week, spending about $500 a month. She takes a taxi to and from work, which costs $350 a month. Shoes and cashmere sweaters take another large chunk. She likes to rent a vacation place in August that has cost as much as $12,000 for the month in past years. She gets her haircuts and color done at a salon that charges $350. And that doesn't include utilities, insurance, groceries, entertainment, household supplies, gifts . . . you get the point. Her net income of just over $7,000 a month is quickly gone. She is baffled and confused at how she got there, and she is truly angry at life. "After all," she says, "I am well respected in my field, I have worked hard to get where I am at my firm, and I earn $120,000 a year—can't I at least afford these few things?" Well, no. By spending the way she has, not only hasn't she been able to afford them, she has accumulated debts totaling $164,000.

"But all my friends spend so much more than I do. Why aren't they in debt? They all own houses and have stock portfolios. Why do they get to spend with impunity and I wind up in debt? My best friend's husband just got a bonus so big they bought a second house and a boat with it. What is wrong with me?"

Pretending doesn't make it so

One of the problems with compulsive spenders and debtors is that they are never very good at estimating what "$120,000 a year" can actually buy. Or what "$50,000 a year" can buy, or "$30,000 a year," or whatever amount a year. They tend to go by a vision in their head of what their income means in terms of what it can buy them. Even then, if that vision doesn't jibe with what they think they "should be able to afford," it is more than likely that they will spend according to that vision, almost as a sort of angry demonstration to the universe that didn't provide it.

Neither is it the case that spenders and debtors tend to be very good at estimating how much they owe. You guessed it—they underestimate. They forget about certain debts. They figure certain ones are paid, when they're not. They figure when it comes down to it, they will go bankrupt, or leave town, or kill themselves—whatever, they'll deal with it later. All manner of fantasies are employed in the effort to justify today. Reality is not a very big component in these psychic figurings. You can almost hear the hurt and disappointed child in all of it, saying, "Why do *they* get to have everything? What about me? I want stuff, too."

Tales of compulsive shopping

Stuff. The rallying cry of compulsive shoppers everywhere. Compulsive shoppers are a little different from other compulsive spenders and debtors. Compulsive shoppers get high from the shopping. They may or may not have the same entitlement problems that rule the overall spending of the compulsive spender or debtor. For them, it's about the shopping. Not that compulsive shoppers buy in order to acquire equity, or that they necessarily need the things they buy. They don't.

Almost without exception, compulsive shoppers don't actually want everything they buy. Their closets are full of clothes with the price tags still attached, their kitchens replete with gadgets that have never been used. Husbands become the beneficiaries of great and varied collections of neckties.

How much money is spent is never the point of compulsive shopping. It is what the shopping fills in for, the obsessive focus of it, the addictive quality to it, that describes the compulsive shopper. Like any intoxicating drug, shopping brings a real adrenaline rush for the compulsive shopper. And, as with a drug, the rush decreases over time, causing the shopper to shop more and more to get that old thrill.

Jill—the perfect excuse: Jill is powerless over the Home Shopping Network. She cannot resist. Even when she is cooking, or cleaning the house, she monitors the television, just in case something comes on that she wouldn't want to miss. None of the patter that the hosts use to entice their audience ever rings fake to her, or ever seems designed simply to part her from her money. She feels more like they are great friends who have found a cache of incredible stuff and are just helping everybody to rummage through this amazing treasure trove.

By any independent measure, Jill's collection of cubic zirconia necklaces and rings, semiprecious brooches and earrings, would seem like a lifetime supply. To Jill, they are all preamble; the next one carries all the emotional weight.

Endlessly complicating matters is the fact that Jill has cancer. She has needed three surgeries and has had all the inevitable radiation, chemo, and terror. Her friends, as friends are wont to do, sympathize, but can't easily find the right words with her. They encourage her to buy whatever will "make her happy," under the general rubric that indulging yourself is what anyone would deserve after the ordeal she's been through. And who could argue with them?

Except Jill knows better. She knows that her compulsive shopping didn't begin when she got cancer. She knows that it has been a theme in her life far longer than that, and that gentle pampering of herself is not what it produces. When the bills start piling up, she doesn't feel pampered at all. She feels doubly cursed.

I suppose you could say that Jill's obsession with buying things from the television is hardly such a terrible thing. Except that she has systematically deprived herself in almost every other area of her life in order to support her habit. She has no money left for taking care of anything except her most basic needs—in fact her shopping obsession has almost totally obscured them. She claims not to really care about going out, taking vacations, or engaging in stimulating or enriching activities. She is totally addicted to her particular form of shopping.

The established pattern of an addiction continuing to claim more and more of a price in ever-expanding areas of life fits Jill's compulsive shopping to a T. Her life outside of work and shopping has become, over time, virtually nonexistent. She has gone whole hog into compulsive debting to support her habit, and her creditors have begun to bear down on her.

Shopping and buying can become a sort of intoxicating reverie insulated from the pressures of the world. "I feel at home when I'm in my favorite store." It is by no means uncommon for compulsive shoppers to feel very real withdrawals when they stop shopping. Shopping is often the one thing that feels totally consistent in their lives.

Jill told me that her father died when she was a teenager, but that before he died, he was very proud to have been able to give her a few small gifts of jewelry. She always cherished them but had forgotten that for a long time.

Compulsive shoppers come in different shapes and sizes. Some are addicted to shoes, to clothes (a lot seem to be addicted to shoes and clothes), to Beanie Babies, to old Barbie dolls, to antiques, to flea markets, to Bloomingdale's, to Big Kmart. It doesn't matter. I know a woman who could no sooner stay home when she knows there's a yard sale than she could change water to wine. Her basement, with only narrow aisles for passage, is literally filled with boxes of stuff that she hasn't looked at in years. The newer stuff is in the attic, but she's running out of room there, too.

I know another woman who spent so much at her favorite store last year that they gave her a Jaguar as a Christmas gift! Another now spends more time on eBay than she does with her job and her family combined. Then there are the shopping bulimics—they buy and buy, then return and return. They don't seem able to savor anything whatsoever, but they cannot stop the self-reinforcing cycle of binge and purge. There is always the aura of guilt about the bulimics. All of them quite different, all so much the same.

Shopping and buying come to substitute for emotional and spiritual longings.

Donna, the debutante shopper: Donna wouldn't be caught dead buying something from the Home Shopping Network. For that matter, she wouldn't even be caught dead buying something from a place she feels is so hopelessly common as, say, Bloomingdale's. Nevertheless, she is far more like Jill than not.

It is a rare week when Donna doesn't go at least once to Neiman

Marcus. It is by no means uncommon for her to go four times. The salespeople all know her by name, and her name is a do-not-forget-to-call when anything new arrives. She feels the store understands her; they know what she likes, and they know how to pamper her (her lunch order is on file—a Cobb salad with dressing on the side, and a herbal iced tea). Last year, she spent a quarter of a million dollars at Neiman's. (But don't get me wrong: Donna is an equal opportunity shopper. She does not discriminate against Barney's, Armani, Prada, or Gucci.)

Donna's closets are filled with clothes she has never worn. In fact, when she redecorated her apartment, extreme attention was paid to the design of the closets. Those who run the hospital thrift shop to which she donates the clothes when she cleans out her closets are as thrilled as they can be when she comes in; most of the tags are still hanging.

But let's admit something immediately: there are lots of people who spend lots of money who are not compulsive shoppers. I'm sure that Donna is not Neiman's biggest customer. I am not sure, however, that their biggest customer is necessarily a compulsive shopper. The amount spent is not the salient feature.

Donna's total savings at any given time are usually less than $10,000. Each of her cashmere shawls costs $3,000.

Occasionally she says, "This is crazy—I have to stop." And she tries with all her ability to avoid spending so much money shopping. She gets scared about living so close to the edge, and regret floods in at having wasted so much money for so long without much to show for it.

Being a compulsive debtor, spender, or shopper is not fun. It may start out that way. Oh, yes. A lot of people report that getting their first credit card, or going on their first shopping spree, felt a lot like getting laid for the first time. A rush of excitement, of intoxication, of power, of taking the edge off, of being initiated into the real world. Come to think of it, addicts are apt to describe their first experience with alcohol or drugs that way, too. Like an addict with his drug, things don't get out of hand right away. Quite the opposite: it feels as if the key to finally being able to negotiate this life has been found. In fact, the spending and borrowing feel just great, thank you very much. Buying stuff, and using credit to live the life you expect, goes right in to fill you up with the sense of wholeness and well-being you were looking for.

But not for long, never for all that long. Over a long enough period, two things eventually happen. The first is that reality starts to crowd in, and living beyond your means takes its natural toll. The other thing that happens, and the more devastating to my mind, is that money and spending and borrowing stop working to make things feel all right. But that doesn't mean you stop the cycle you're in. That's the problem with addictive cycles—you don't stop.

Once you are stuck in an obsessive or addictive money cycle, money and worry begin to form a continual loop in your mind. A huge amount of time and psychic space are taken up with worrying and obsessing about money and debt and work. As debt grows and becomes unmanageable, it gets hard to ignore the consequences that begin adding up: payments don't get made on time, collection agents start calling, lawsuits are threatened—depression sets in. Fantasies take hold about a big score, or an ultimate bailout.

Compulsive spenders and debtors are ruled by a unique sense of entitlement. They cannot accept life on life's terms.

Warning signs that things will not end well begin fairly early. They just get ignored, pushed down as deep as they'll go. But they don't stay there; the warnings get more and more urgent, and they start to come a lot more frequently. Elaborate explanations and justifications are employed to keep them away, if only for just a little bit longer.

Compulsive spenders and debtors even pretend sometimes that there is no real problem. They continually try to reframe their debt as a temporary problem, not a frightening and growing theme in their life. They rationalize for as long as they possibly can that it is manageable. They get more credit cards, they borrow from Peter to pay Paul, they put off the day of reckoning for as long as it is humanly possible. Maybe in their most lucid moments they see things more clearly, but it is hard to hold on to those insights.

Workaholism

Workaholics create a cocoon for themselves. Instead of a safe place where they hide from life, in this case it's a more complex way of hiding from themselves. Workaholics tend to buy their own cover story: that all the zeal and commitment and intensity they bring to their work *is all about the work*. The obsession with work is maintained because workaholism is simply called something else—ambition, competition, a well-developed work ethic, responsibility to family, building a business, making partner at the firm, meeting the demands of the job, protecting yourself from losing your job—the list is endless. That the work itself is the addiction is hidden under an avalanche of culturally accepted reasons for overworking.

Workaholics use work to keep feelings at bay and to lock away deeper needs and desires. When you are in an obsessive cycle with work, the focus is always on an ambiguous goal in the future, the "pot of gold." It is easier to live in that fantasy than to deal with today. When you are living in a state of pure potential, you don't have to set down solidly in today, and you become adept at avoiding coming to grips with inner reality and everyday life.

I don't mean to say that workaholics don't work to earn money, or to get recognition, or to achieve their stated goals. Of course they do. But deeper needs are what truly animate the addicted worker. The things a workaholic works for, and the things a nonaddictive worker works for, seem exactly the same on the surface. But underneath they are as different as night and day.

Work substitutes for meaning. It supplies purpose, which might otherwise be missing in action.

Barbara—a home away from home: Everyone knows not to call Barbara at home. The reason is that you can never find her there. No matter what time you're calling, you try her at the office.

She pretty much grew up on her own. Her parents traveled all through her childhood, and she was mainly reared by an aunt and uncle who were understanding but not emotionally available to her.

Barbara works a whole lot more than most people. Work is the only thing that feels absolutely real to her. She feels as if work is a self-contained world with all the comforts of home—coffee, snacks, family fights, best buddies, grudges, crushes, you-name-it. She doesn't take very many days off, and she doesn't exactly know what she would do with them if she did. She works most Saturdays. She doesn't really like to admit it, but she works most Sundays, too. None of her friends actually expects her to show up for any plans they make; they have become inured to her well-meaning but inevitably broken promises. When she makes it out to dinner with them during the week (she tries, she tells them, she really tries), she rushes back to the office as if she had told someone at work she was just slipping out to buy the newspaper.

Barbara works in public relations. She says she really loves the kind of work that she does, and by all accounts, she is extremely good at it. Indispensable is the kind of word people use to describe her. If you ask her why she works such long hours or with such intensity, she is likely to tell you that everyone at her office works that way, that the special projects are coming faster these days, or that she really likes feeling indispensable. Barbara loves to talk about how much overtime she gets, and how her dinners and taxis are paid for when she works so late. She feels taken care of, she says. She has been working at this pace for nine years now.

Her rationale for how intensely she works, and for all the long hours, is deceptive, because it is always subject to change. There is never a time when she feels as though she can take it easy for a while—no matter what. Barbara didn't reduce her hours one bit when she was promoted this year, although she no longer qualified for over-time pay. In all honesty, she says, she may have increased them. New reasons became immediately clear to her why she couldn't possibly work less—the work wouldn't get done, she would appear ungrateful, and in any case the only way to keep getting ahead is to keep working like a maniac (the rallying cry of workaholics everywhere). Is that true? No real time was given over to reflect on the question; it was taken as an article of faith.

Craig and the illusion of control: Workaholics are particularly adept at maintaining justifiable reasons for their intense and obsessive working. One favorite is that working as they do is the only way to get ahead and stay ahead. Another is the old chestnut about working like a demon until a certain time, or until achieving a certain goal, when they will really be able to kick back and relax. But does anyone actually know of a workaholic who became spontaneously able to kick back and relax? And, of course, there is the all-time favorite reason for addictive working—to make money. But again, does anyone really stop their workaholism because of earning a certain amount of money?

If there is any doubt that workaholics work to protect against unwanted feelings, just look at a workaholic when he tries to relax, or to stay away from work for an extended period of time. Have you ever seen anyone more uncomfortable? It seems as if they are under attack from some unseen but terribly agitating force.

Craig makes a serious amount of money. He is the source of a lot of envy among his friends, and he likes it that way. He grew up in a family where the measure of the man was the measure of his bank account. It was always very clear who was revered in the family (the rich ones), and who was deemed a failure (all the others).

Craig works right through his meals—he either skips them or has them at his desk. And make no mistake, Craig is at his desk for all three meals. You get a sense that he would gladly sleep in his Aeron chair, at his desk, if his wife would give her blessing. Speaking of his wife, when she finally convinced him to take a vacation last summer, he sat on the beach at Amagansett with a satellite phone attached to the modem on his laptop, doing business, always doing business. Asked about what he makes of it all, he says, "I looked around. I know I was the only one with a satellite command center on the beach. What can I do? That's who I am."

Craig is the executive vice president of a multinational corporation. He also happens to run a hedge fund from his desk there. He likes to joke that he's on the lookout for a third job to complete the hat trick he never did get to score in varsity hockey. He is penetratingly intelligent. He is hyperalert. And he is happiest when there are several difficult calculations to make instantly. You get the feeling that Craig was given extra rations on the day they gave out the adrenaline. In his mind, each of his jobs requires about sixty hours a week, and that is just fine by his reckoning.

It is not that he is without support staff; he has very capable assistants and managers, but he does not actually let them do very much, except tend to his manic needs. With a phalanx of monitors in a semicircle, and a row of phones covering the "L" part of his desk—he looks as if he sits at Strategic Air Command. Because he gets anxious when he has to wait even a second, he had a T-3 Internet connection installed—also making it possible to download the *Encyclopaedia Britannica* in a couple of seconds if he ever had a mind to.

The women at the office all seem to pamper and protect him. All right, it's true, they all pretty much want to have an affair with him, too (he is, after all, rich and powerful, not to mention handsome and very charming). Craig does his flirting in a more subtle, wielding-of-power and showing-of-attention way, but he is right in there with them. After all, workaholics turn to work for the meaning in their life, so it is by no means a surprise when they look there to meet romantic needs, too.

Craig has amassed five times the amount of money that he once thought of as his "magic number." Not unlike workaholics everywhere, he justified his incredibly intense work style, and outrageous work hours, by having a plateau he was working toward, a time when he would have all the money he would ever need; a time when he could enjoy the good life from then on. But it is a myth. That is not what Craig or any other workaholic really works for.

I asked him why he didn't retire when he reached his magic number. He had no real answer. The real answer is that no workaholic does. The magic number is a beautifully designed excuse to keep the addictive work going and justified. Once a magic number is achieved, and usually long before that, a newer, bigger number takes its place. Every plateau is replaced with some new idea of when it would all stop. But any fantasy about a magic number or a magic day are conjured, make no mistake, in the service of *continuing the work*, not stopping it.

Workaholics don't feel stigmatized—they're proud of the way they work

You won't have very much trouble getting a workaholic to admit to being one, until they have traveled very far down the road. Working doesn't feel like a problem, it feels like a solution. They don't really view being a workaholic as an "admission" at all, since they tend to wear the title with a certain amount of pride. "Workaholic," if you ask them, means something like "Someone who is dedicated; a tough competitor. They'll do whatever it takes to get the job done. A workaholic is most definitely someone who is destined to get ahead further and faster than those who aren't willing to work with full gusto." In today's lexicon, the word seems almost to have lost its original meaning as someone who is addicted to work, not someone who is good at or dedicated to their work. There is a profound difference between the two.

Much like compulsive shoppers who are proud of their newest finds, workaholics pride themselves on how much work they do and on how much stamina and drive they have. "Yeah, I work about seventy hours a week. But during an incredible crunch time recently, I worked close to a hundred hours a week for an entire month." The man who told me that was not describing the depths of his problem, he was describing a sort of conquest. Workaholics are buffeted by a giant wave of cultural approval. Work is, in that sense, the perfect addiction.

Endlessly complicating matters for the workaholic is that money and power are compelling and intoxicating all by themselves, thank you very much. The workaholic in his cups is often drunk not only on the energy he brings to his work and on the work's diversion from himself, but on money and power, too. Working hard and long to establish a safe and secure future is seen as such a benign, honorable goal that workaholics tend to hide behind it with impunity.

This thing doesn't get better with time, it gets worse: The ante always gets upped. The same amount of work and intensity will not get the job done as time goes by. All of a sudden there are newer and higher levels to be maintained. Linda has been upping the ante for quite some time. By now, she is spinning like a top.

Linda is so full of energy that even the first words in her sentences sound like they are from the middle of heated arguments. She launches into thoughts with reckless abandon. If you like it, she elaborates. If not, in half a second, she's on to the next. It's hard to imagine that she actually sleeps. Come to think of it, she doesn't sleep all that much. Linda is a workaholic of the first order. If she wakes up later than five A.M., she feels guilty. There are long periods when she's *at her desk* at five A.M. I know what you might be thinking; she's a West Coast stockbroker and has to be up for the opening of the markets and goes home at two P.M. No way. Neither is she in the dairy business. No, she works, and she works hard, until at least nine every night. As often as not she works until midnight.

The amazing thing is that Linda jam-packs a million things besides work into her schedule, too. She doesn't do all the things she schedules, but damned if she doesn't believe she will. If you were to join her for one of these other activities you would soon understand. She puts you in mind of nothing so much as that incredible kind of housefly that lives its entire life without ever landing. Linda belongs to a gym, but her workout schedule doesn't leave even one minute for getting there, changing, or getting back. "How could I?" she says. "If I admit it takes that much time I would never be able to go." Linda is a power shopper, and no one is more up-to-date on what's hot and what's not. You cannot discuss an article from a magazine that she hasn't read, or a piece of gossip she hasn't heard. The phone at her desk—for her use only—has six lines.

Linda is a highly intelligent and extremely accomplished woman. She is the president of the division of the company she works for. Not only has no woman ever been named president before, no one as young as she, man or woman, has ever been named president before. She has used her supercharged work energy to propel her through successive promotions and coups. She seems to be able to do whatever she sets her mind to.

What she is not able to do is stop. What she cannot do is relax. Relax? She doesn't even stop thinking and worrying about everything long enough to consider relaxing. Last summer she was talked into taking a house in the Hamptons. I don't think you would say she got value for her money. She went out for the weekend a total of eight times. Two of those times she came back the same day she went out—

something about an emergency at work. Which hardly matters very much, since when she did stay, she was constantly working at her laptop or taking calls on the cell phone. She went to the beach exactly twice (and she was antsy those two times). In any case, it should be noted that she went to a beach where, she had heard, most of the other people from her industry went. In other words: it hardly matters, Hamptons or New York, work or beach—it's all the same.

The truth is that workaholism may keep the workaholic from herself, but it hardly keeps her from achieving surface goals. In fact, workaholics tend to do even better in that race than their nonaddicted counterparts, thereby setting up a self-reinforcing system that tells them everything must be going just fine. That is the confusing part. To a great degree, everyone wants what workaholics say they want: success at their work, recognition for a job well done, and financial rewards for their efforts. And, even more confusingly, a lot of people use similar methods to achieve those goals. But work addiction is not characterized by how many hours are worked, or by how intensely those hours are spent, or by how much is accomplished. It is characterized by the work being driven by deeper needs.

Work is the thing workaholics rely on to provide themselves with a sense of well-being: "I always felt more at home at the office than I did at home." While it is still spinning its magic, work feels great; otherwise no one would get addicted to it—people get addicted to things that make them feel good, not bad. It may be one of the only things in life that does. "Work gives me such a feeling of satisfaction. I wish I could say the same about the rest of my life." The problem is that the situation doesn't last. No addiction keeps working as it once did. What was your best friend turns on you, leaving in its wake a terrible feeling of emptiness and longing.

Robert and Julie, working it out: Robert and Julie fell in love quickly. He was an investment banker; she was a honcho at an advertising agency. They had that warm, oceanic feeling of having known each other forever, of being so automatically in sync. They both came from traditional families, and they both worked crazy hours. Sixty, seventy, eighty hours a week. They loved squeezing their dates into their busy schedules. Falling in love would be no reason for slacking off: neither movies, nor theater, nor Chinese food, nor weekends in the country stayed these lovers from the swift completion of their appointed rounds.

Once they were married, Robert envisioned working to take care of a family, and he already had the idea that any wife of his should be at home tending to the house they would buy and the kids they would have, and to spending the fortune he would make.

And work he did. Very quickly indeed, Robert's stock began to rise at the firm. And at the firm where he works, when your stock rises, big money follows. He was a millionaire at thirty-two. When Julie got pregnant, Robert was very clear: his wife would not return to work. All the work that ever needed to be done for his family, he was more than willing to do (demanded to do, really). He told Julie to quit her job, and to start looking for a suitable apartment large enough to house the new life of Mr. and Mrs. Robert Workington.

With everything settled in his mind, Robert's single-minded focus on work allowed little room for anything else. He was never home. Many months went by during which he came home only for a few hours to sleep, or take a shower. Pursuing certain high-profile deals, he stayed out of town for six to eight weeks at a time. When Julie asked why she didn't see him anymore, he told her that he had to make partner, and in his mind that covered a multitude of sins. Once he became partner, the implication went, that's when there would be time for everything. Julie knew he was only kidding himself. Once you're on the work-go-round, you don't get off when you make partner. You get off when you are ready to get off.

Each time a new partnership list came out and Robert's name failed to be on it, he redoubled his efforts. He used his anger as fuel. Robert found a deal to concentrate on that was by far the most demanding yet. Julie, who by this time had two toddlers, began to think that not only was he a workaholic in high gear but that he was cheating on her as well (although to the best of my knowledge that was never true). Either that or he simply didn't love her anymore.

Jane can't put relax on her to do list: Once they have a glimmer that their relationship to work is not exactly as it seems, workaholics try innumerable ways to prove to themselves that they are just fine, that the way they work is not their problem. They sign up at the gym, get away for weekends, or take a house at the beach. They force themselves to relax, maybe take a yoga class. But they sort of stink at those things. It is hard to get the benefit from a yoga class when you are powering your way through it as one thing on a list of five million things to do.

Eventually, compulsive workers come face-to-face with their problem: the feelings that were being kept at bay by all the compulsive activity start refusing to stay away. They demand to have their day in the light. And, boy, do workaholics ever tolerate this badly. They aren't exactly known for having developed a capacity to deal with flooding feelings. At the same time, the capacity to relax, never high on the compulsive worker's list of priorities, becomes nearly impossible to access.

Jane has been trying to relax for years. She is a power workaholic, but for her, admitting that would mean she has to do something about it. And she does not want to stop what has felt like her lifeline, the thing she has come to depend on absolutely. The problem is that none of her old tricks seems to work very well anymore. She is a physician, and she works as many hours, probably with greater intensity than ever, but she can't shake the feeling of emptiness. She feels afraid. Every time she is able to unhook from the work machine, she gets intolerably anxious, as if an old enemy has finally found her.

Jane has been exercising, except that she compulsively schedules the exercise in a way that makes the rest of her overflowing schedule even more tense. All of a sudden there's dance class, yoga, personal trainers, spinning classes—moderation has never been an arrow in the workaholic quiver. She has determined to spend more time with friends, to enjoy her social life. She seems, though, to approach it in a way that leaves her either totally overscheduled with friends and even more stressed out, if that is possible, or she has to absolutely withdraw from them because she doesn't have an ounce of energy left.

The problem is that she has added all these things to her schedule but hasn't cut back on working at all. The idea that there are a limited number of hours and a limited amount of energy is not one that she is ready to accept. Certainly 168 hours in a week isn't enough to her—unless somehow she didn't have to sleep.

At the end of the day, through all her trying to relax and expand her life, the problem remains that she feels useful only when she is working. She no longer gets the jolt of energy or the solid sense of identity that work used to provide, but she still hasn't found a way to work any less. She just feels worse while she does it.

I know I've said it before, but here goes again: because what is sought is not what is missing, what is found is not what is needed. No matter how much is found. No number of square pegs can ever fit in that round hole, and that is why an obsessive pattern like workaholism always gets worse, never better.

Money Obsession

You can certainly be in an obsessive pattern with money without falling firmly into the categories of overspender, underearner, or workaholic. I'm talking about people whose thoughts, worries, and desires center on money. Their lives revolve around money, they can't stop thinking about it, all else is automatically relegated to second place. Money is their obsession.

Money is a mood-changer for most people, at least some of the time, but not everyone falls into an addictive pattern with it. It's much the same as with alcohol; everyone gets a buzz from a drink, but to an alcoholic, it's not just a buzz. It's what they've been looking for, a way to be in the world. Money can fill the same void.

It can hardly be a surprise that there are more and more money-holics. In a time when money has become the lens through which we view ourselves and construct the narratives of who we are, you can almost say we are *breeding* a certain tendency to money addiction. When did money become so central to our thoughts about ourselves?

Tony, switching obsessions: Tony resigned from his job recently. "Who would stay there when you're making the kind of money I am in the stock market?" Tony had been the vice president of sales for a large manufacturing company. He was earning nearly $300,000 per year. He had started out as a poor kid, and he was the first in his family to "make it big." Along the way, he got hooked on being part of the big time.

He was jet propelled. He rose from salesman to sales manager to vice president in a few short years. Once he started making "real money," the idea that he might be able to have what he considered a very real fortune took up residence in his head. Numbers, and how much it meant to be rich, became the focus of his obsessive thinking. With each new level of earning, the amount of money he needed to feel rich seemed to recede further and further instead of coming closer. Not that he didn't have substantial savings—he did. He saved far more than he ever spent. He had remained single and had somewhat less than extravagant tastes. Nevertheless, money and everything to do with money were his obsession. He wanted to be the guy people were in awe of when he came into the room, because everyone would know how incredibly rich he was.

His dabbling in the market became full-fledged once he made his first big hit. He had bought some shares of an IPO based on the recommendation of a friend, and they tripled in less than a week. I believe you could say he was hooked at the moment he saw that profit booked to his brokerage account. More than $30,000, just like that. Eight months later he walked into his boss's office and quit. He couldn't spare the time away from his new all-consuming passion. The next day, he was set up at home with every financial information service known to man piped into his computer. Tony may now be the premier expert on food delivered to your desk on the Upper East Side of New York City: since he set up his computer trading system at home, he doesn't leave his desk. Not during market hours, anyway. And not for the many hours he spends poring over reports and financial news, nor for the hours spent plugging into his expanding network of equally intense investing colleagues, none of whom he has ever actually met.

Tony has become a virtual recluse. When he does leave the house now it's usually at night, and you could forgive the casual observer for getting the idea that he had just slipped out of his sarcophagus for a stroll. He hasn't kept in touch with the friends he made at his old job, nor does he seem to care about establishing a new social life. He can't remember the last time he went on a date. But he is making money. And he does count his money—leaving the distinct impression that soon a group of Dickensian ghosts might be arriving.

Windfall fantasies: the great American dream

Fantasies about windfalls, "life-changing money," may be the new American Dream. "When I get two million together, you won't see me darkening a doorway where people work anymore." "Four million—when I hit four million, it's good-bye to this grind, and hello Caribbean sailboat." I know a man who recently cashed in an investment that brought him a profit of $17 million; he is now obsessed with having $100 million (that's the amount he is convinced really rich people have these days).

Let's look at what really happens to people when the fantasy comes true. The purest fruition of the windfall fantasy is hitting the lottery. Except lottery winners report that the experience of winning was nothing like they thought it would be. None of the feelings was as they expected; no heightened sense of security, no catharsis, and most of all, except for a very brief thrill—no feeling of real happiness or satisfaction. Actually, they say their lives take on a sort of frantic quality. When you hear lottery winners describe what their life was like after they won, it is not Easy Street they talk about. The truth is this: an astonishing number of lottery winners never really feel very comfortable again, and it is by no means uncommon for lottery winners to eventually wind up in bankruptcy court. Two of the biggest stressors in life are a sudden and large decrease in finances, and a sudden and large increase in finances. You guessed it, the bigger stress actually comes from the sudden *increase.*

It is a lonely day when you realize that the thing you thought would deposit you in a state of bliss instead leaves you cold. Lottery winners tell about how alienated and alone they feel. They feel that everyone wants something from them. They say they feel as if they bring out people's unbridled envy. Something happens that they would not have believed if you had sworn it on a stack of Bibles— they long for the days before they won. The days when they still felt connected to the earth. And none of the expensive toys that they buy in search of the ecstatic feeling they expected produces the desired results.

It is not very much different for the high-flying executive who makes partner, or who finally gets the million-dollar bonus check he's been hoping for his whole life. True, he is not as likely to subsequently go bankrupt, but the disillusionment that comes on the heels of getting what you always wanted, and having it feel nothing like you expected it to, *is exactly the same as the lottery winners' experience.*

Peter and what he lost along the way: Trading bonds at a rarefied level for one of Wall Street's biggest investment firms, Peter became a millionaire at twenty-eight. Shortly after his thirtieth birthday he received a one-year-bonus check of nearly $3 million. The surprising thing is what happened next—staring at the check in his hand, he began to cry.

Something seemed clear at that moment that had never found its way to the front of his consciousness before. He had what he always wanted, but all he felt was what was missing, how much he had foreclosed on in the rest of his life during his single-minded pursuit.

Intimate relationships? Suddenly he wasn't sure he had even a nodding acquaintance with them. He was not close to his family: they reminded him of his humble beginnings and made him feel a little embarrassed. In the romantic realm, he fell into the cynical view of his peers: relationships were just so much commerce. "The more beautiful the woman is, the richer the man has to be in order to attract her."

Peter's lifelong goal had been to become rich. To have serious money. Coming from a working-class family, he had, of course, long ago surpassed any original idea of how much serious money might be. Peter wears a $24,000 wristwatch, and in his milieu the difference between a $10,000 watch and one worth $24,000 might mean the difference between feeling good about yourself and not. The weekly tab for his dinners with a group of four of his buddies regularly runs as high as $1,000, and not many have won out in the fight with Peter for the check.

Having achieved his dream of money, he imagined he would feel a deep sense of well-being, maybe even a feeling of invulnerability—a sort of natural bliss. He was rich. How could he have been so wrong about what that might mean? He came to think that the problem was actually a simple one—that his notion of being rich was minor league, forged in his working-class background, that he was just a piker in the world of real money and that all he need do was redouble his efforts. After all, guys around him were making his money look like pin money. He couldn't begin to afford a beachfront Southampton house or a private jet. Maybe the price of admission to the dream had simply been raised while he wasn't looking.

All money disorders have at their core the same thing: something missing in the emotional and spiritual realm. An imbalance that is ever trying to right itself. These disorders are an attempt, even if guided by an illusion, at emotional self-medication. Money is perceived as a sort of all-purpose replacement for what is missing. None of this is a conscious process, but it rules the day more than any conscious process ever could.

The long bull market of the nineties gave rise to an enormous increase in individuals owning stock and making their own investment decisions and has bred a whole new generation of moneyholics. They are the ones who have become glued to computer screens, obsessively watching their stock prices. They are the ones desperate to beat the S&P 500, the leading composite indexes, to prove they are winning the game. I frequent a drugstore where, if the stock market is open, it can be reliably predicted that the pharmacist will be on the phone with his broker. The counterman at the deli where I get sandwiches proffers stock tips to some of his better customers.

Stanley's money doesn't take away the fear of financial insecurity: Then there are the disillusioned ones. I'm talking about people who are on the other side of the equation. Their obsession is more about what the hell happened to their lives. About wondering why money didn't pan out the way it was supposed to. Trust-funders are an especially revealing group, with the double-barreled shot of expectation and guilt, who are famously troubled by the money that is theirs. Somehow being freely given what everyone else is striving for is crazy-making.

Stanley had a sizable trust fund. He was also lucky enough to have invested a large portion of it in New York real estate at just the right time. He has an amount of money that 99 percent of all people would say they could never spend in a lifetime. Which does not temper at all his dreadful worry, all the time, that he is running out of money. The one thing that he is sure of is this: he doesn't have enough money.

Maybe he doesn't. Stanley leads the life of a country gentleman in the city. He and his current wife live in an apartment overlooking Central Park. Their "summer cottage" is on the beach in the Hamptons, and the whole family, including all the household help, repairs for a month at Christmas to the Palm Beach manse.

His children attend the most exclusive schools. His wife owns the most exclusive horses. And he donates large philanthropic sums. But although he gives very grand amounts, he oddly, and oftentimes, extends his largesse far beyond his original intent. He wants to feel as if he can bestow any amount, and he doesn't understand why he likes it so much when people think he is even richer than he is.

Stanley does not work. He spends his time at elegant lunches. And he is on a certain high-flung social circuit. If you were to ask people their perception of Stanley, they would inevitably describe him as refined, self-assured, and caring. The self-assured part is a matter of perception. Stanley feels anything but self-assured. He is worried most of the time. He receives about $3.5 million per year from his investments. He spends $5.5 million. At the current rate, he estimates he will be completely broke in twelve years. And the current rate keeps increasing.

Stanley is sixty-six, maybe he'll make the money last. But he has plans to leave a fortune to his children, and his younger wife doesn't seem like someone who is very much interested in economizing. When trying to get to sleep, the thing that has been helping Stanley the most these days is imagining a windfall of new money. Sometimes the fantasy works, sometimes it doesn't. With all his friends so much richer than he is, his imaginings range to the hundreds of millions just to feel competitive. Incredibly, Stanley lives his life in fear. We had lunch together recently. "Why haven't you ordered your usual Perrier?" I asked. Without a hint of irony he replied, "I can't afford it."

It just may be that simply having a sizable trust fund is diagnostic as a money disorder. It is certainly a well-known dynamic that people with such funds struggle with their sense of self, and with finding their way in the world, free from the shadow of their legacy. The struggle to establish a purpose in their life, and to find meaning while struggling against expectation, is inherently difficult for trust-funders.

This is certainly the case with Will, who has never worked a day in his life. He announced that proudly when we met. Strangely, he has also told me that he thinks he would be a workaholic if he ever did work. Will inherited money from a famous father, and he has used it to create a cocoon of luxury, insulated from the high expectations and inevitable comparisons to his illustrious father. He is a confirmed bachelor. He is not a monk. His restaurant bill (he very much likes taking the women he knows to lunch) generally comes to about $7,000 per month.

He renovated his penthouse apartment with such precision that he lived in a hotel for nearly two years while it was carried out. He turned the bedroom into a sort of custom-made fortress against the world. It has heavily reinforced walls insulated with soundproofing. The wide-screen television takes up the entire wall in front of the bed. His computer is right at hand, as are the numbers of all the stores he frequents. He likes to think he could live there very comfortably for as long as he ever wants to.

Whenever the buzz gets buzzing about some new type of therapy, Will signs up. He went to Mind Control in the sixties, and est in the seventies. He twelve-stepped the eighties, and New-Aged the nineties. He has screamed primally, and purged colonically; he has been cleansed, fasted, and meditated. He is in private as well as group psychoanalysis.

But he feels empty. I have never met anyone who seeks so much and finds so little. He wishes his money came from his own efforts. He wishes he were held in esteem by a group of peers instead of a group of headwaiters. He wishes he had finished school, perhaps gotten an advanced degree. He wishes he didn't feel degraded every time he has to ask his mother for money to supplement his very substantial income (as he sometimes finds it necessary to do). Mostly, he wishes he were living his own life, instead of the one that money has him living.

In his private moments, when the lights are low, he wishes he had the courage to renounce his legacy. To loose the tie that binds him to his long dead but overbearing father. To test his mettle. But it is also in those moments when he has admitted to himself that he cannot. And there he is, in his very luxurious fortress.

Amanda and the curse of inheritance: What is it about money that drives some people to desperately wish they had it some other way? How surprising it is to most people when the obsession with money comes from having far too much of it for comfort. A great deal of money can seem an onerous burden if there isn't a safe psychic place to put it. The sense of self necessary to accept less than you imagined you would have is just as necessary to accept more than anyone could ever need.

Amanda inherited a fortune from both sides of her family. Deep money. She got a few million when she turned eighteen, five times that at twenty-one. At thirty she got the real money. Instead of feeling blessed, Amanda felt cursed.

Outrageous money; outrageous rebellion. It was as if she were a comic character in a strip called "Rich Kid Rebels." We're not just talking about putting off embracing her legacy for a while, while she sowed a few wild oats. No. Amanda took up residence in an apartment that refugees from the Third World would turn down on principle. Her clothes weren't thrift shop chic, they were thrift shop junk.

She hung out at rock clubs and took heroin. Pretty soon she was strung out. And loving it. Living as a junkie was the neo plus ultra of rejecting her parents and everything they stood for. A sort of inverse money dream took shape—by *not* having it, she could build a fortress around herself. Just like those who labor under the misconception that money will somehow shield them from the world, Amanda thought somehow that rejecting it would do the same. It doesn't work that way either.

Heroin hastened her decline. Maybe that was her salvation. Recovering from drug addiction forced her to focus on her relationship to her wealth. She was ashamed of her station as surely as anyone who had grown up without enough food. Uncomfortable in her own skin, she said. If only she could shed the intolerable burden she felt weighed down beneath.

But there is no right amount of money to have. No amount to shield you from the world, or turn you into the person you hope to be.

Still profoundly uncomfortable with her great wealth, she struggled with the meaning of that head-on. What does it mean to have enough money to take care of anything you could ever want? Or, for that matter, anything your children and their children could ever want? Do any responsibilities go with that? Is there a moral bearing on decisions on how to spend your money? Can a plan for spending your money help to express your values, dreams, and desires? What about the ancient practice of tithing? Amanda started asking these questions.

When we live in an unbridled quest for money, as if money is the answer, we make the mistake of confusing the symbol for what is symbolized. The dream of money turns out to be more like an illusion than a dream. But it is an illusion that is rooted deep in popular culture, and deep in our collective psyche. The longing for money, the illusion that it can provide anything, and all the emotional freight it carries for us provide enough power and urgency to fuel our lust for it. What is obscured in all this is the saddest part of all—that money is not what our soul is longing for to begin with—it is the things that money represents to us that we truly long for. Like love, security, connection, validation, and faith.

The Underearners

The scope of money disorders has expanded to include underearning, more or less parallel to the way eating disorders eventually came to include anorexia and bulimia. The syndromes with the most obvious symptoms—overspending, workaholism, and obsession—were identified and understood first, just as compulsive overeating was understood prior to anorexia or "undereating." And the two phenomena are fairly analogous—both the money disorder and the eating disorder have much the same goal: to stay as small as possible in order to deny desire, to feel safe and in control. They also have much the same *modus operandi*: underearners and anorectics alike exert extreme control over their world in an effort to dispel anxiety. The main arrow in their quiver is called deprivation.

If you are not an underearner, the ways that underearners go about their lives seem frustrating, counterintuitive. What might make someone overspend makes sense at least a little bit to just about everyone. But what makes someone, consciously or not, conspire to keep small, hidden, out of view, is a more mysterious process.

Deprivation is like a world with certain colors missing. Chronic underearning and anorectic spending are adaptive responses to living in a world that feels too damn scary. They are subconscious devices, that struggle to reconcile the outer world with an inner world of fears and doubts about ourselves and our abilities. Underearning and anorectic spending are essentially protective measures, meant to insulate, to form a very real barrier, against rejection, competition, and envy. Underearners do not do well with rejection, competition, or envy. They do not do well with advocating on their own behalf either.

It is not merely a bit of bad luck when a woman with two Ph.D.s cannot, for the life of her, find a way to earn a living wage. Similarly, it is not for a lack of clients who are willing to pay competitive fees that an accomplished freelance engineer has never been able to earn anywhere near what his experience and talent might be realistically expected to bring. Neither can it be called simply modest living when a man tries to spend less and less every week so that he can get down to what he calls his "lowest possible living expenses."

Underearning is not about low income, it's about low self-esteem

Underearning is not defined by how much money is being earned, or not earned. There is a world of difference between someone who is not earning very much right now, or whose abilities are limited, and the chronic underearner. Underearners don't underearn because the world doesn't pay them enough. They underearn because they subconsciously *find a way* for the world not to pay them enough. They have an uncanny knack for sabotaging their own efforts, or for simply devaluing them from the start. Even when they finally muster the energy or the courage to go out and assert themselves, they always seem to be driving with the brakes on.

Ellen is a freelance designer with an impressive portfolio. Although she is accomplished at her art, and her work has appeared in major magazines and newspapers, she never earns a living wage. Even when she was on staff, she was paid much less than the others at her company. She never asked for a raise. Ellen never has any money to spend on herself, and her savings are always ridiculously, perilously low. When I met her, she was without health insurance, she needed a new winter coat, and she had come to see going to the movies as a scary waste of money. "What happens if I run out of money?" she asked. "I'll tell you what happens. I will wish I hadn't gone to the damned movies. That's what happens."

Ellen is extremely intelligent, creative, and Ivy League educated, and you get the feeling she is a sensitive and caring person. But when you talk to her, especially about earning a living or taking care of herself, a fog seems to roll into the room and hang between you. It is as if only some of her vibrancy, intelligence, and creativity is ever allowed to see the light of day. The rest is always kept firmly and confusingly under wraps. This is true even when she feels she has thrown caution to the wind. (I'm speaking in her terms, of course—I don't think that by any independent measure Ellen can ever be said to have thrown caution to the winds.)

She says she is baffled by the way other people seem to be able to just make money. It is a mystery to her how it all seems so easy to them, how they seem to naturally handle themselves in the business world. Ellen doesn't experience things that way; she can't stop thinking about how she should present herself, about what people must think of her and how unlikely they are to choose her, about how to keep her negative thinking out of the room, and about why things are always so damned hard for her. When she gets the opportunity to go after really great work, she shies away, afraid that presuming she might actually be considered for such positions would call out an angry deity, or at least that she would finally be found out as a fraud. Or, on the off chance that she gets a plum assignment, she then can't see her way clear to having the plum assignment *and asking for enough money to make the thing profitable to her.*

When she told me how much she spends on food per month, I figured most people spend that in a week. Ellen's underearning and deprivation have had their fingers around her throat for as long as she can remember. But you don't have to spend very much time around her to sense that her own deepest belief is that she isn't worth any more than she gets.

There is usually a fair amount of dissonance between what an underearner wants and works toward and what their psychic economy wants and works toward. They are at cross-purposes. The surface self wants to get ahead, to prosper, and to build a stable professional life. But in the deeper reaches, there is a battle going on to keep the world as small and as safe as possible so as to avoid disappointment—which feels sort of like dying to the underearner. It is abundantly clear which self tends to win the day.

When you shut down desire, you always overshoot the mark

Staying small so that the world won't see fit to lop off your head once you stick it out is the tried and true underlying theme of the underearner. Shutting down desires so you won't feel disappointed at not getting what you want is the primary tool. When you set out to shut down your desires, you never shut down only the things you aimed to. All of a sudden, you find you've shut down all sorts of things you hadn't intended; the shutting down spills over into your appetite for food, for sex, for intimacy—the very appetite for living a vital and involved life.

The main fear is that there isn't enough in the world, no way to feel taken care of. The idea that the universe is abundant is not subscribed to, or if it is, it can feel doubly cruel since the main thought then is "What happened to my part of all the abundance?" The natural reaction is to spend as little as possible, to conserve whatever resources there are. Going on vacation becomes out of the question. Vacation? Going to the movies can be a really big deal. Buying Kleenex instead of the store brand can come to feel like a dangerous level of indulgence. I know an underearner who was proud of getting his food expenses down to seven dollars one week.

Underearners become very cozy in their little caves. They know how to deal with deprivation, it's theirs, and they have learned that very well, thank you. It is abundance that scares the hell out of them. You can almost hear them saying, "If I keep my profile small enough, I won't catch the attention of the scary world out there." Even when underearners do have some financial abundance come their way, they tend to feel distinctly uncomfortable about it. They either can't bring themselves to spend any of it for things they want, or they spend it quickly and without much thought. Or, they feel they didn't really deserve the abundance in the first place, and can't seem to contain all the feelings that go along with that. If a sudden windfall happens, especially an inheritance, it can even precipitate a plunge into depression.

The idea of having a sense of plenty, security, and abundance, and then losing it, is far scarier to an underearner than never having had it in the first place.

Kelly—underearners would rather never have than have and then lose: Kelly grew up in a family of great privilege and was schooled in the manner of wealth and luxury. The truth of their income, however, meant that she and her mother did not have the money to live in grand style after the divorce, even though everyone seemed to expect them to. Instead, they affected a sort of shabby gentility.

Kelly did brilliantly in school. Out in the work world, however, she did not fare quite so well. Kelly felt she either deserved to be as rich as she was meant to be by birthright—or she could do without money at all, thank you very much. So she lived mostly without any money at all. She pretended money didn't mean anything to her. A pretty effective defense, I suppose, since she couldn't seem to earn very much. Her difficulty owning her natural talent meant it was hard to find a job, or to believe she could do well at it. Her feelings of entitlement meant that once she had a job, she always felt as if the job was beneath her, and she invariably lost it, or quit first before she could get fired again. Somehow or other there was never enough money to pay the bills for the month.

None of the jobs she worked at seemed like jobs she would even apply for. It was as if she were looking for jobs for a friend of hers with totally different interests and talents. Even when she did finally land a job she liked and was good at, with a fashion designer, she sabotaged it by allowing people to take advantage of her. She then became so resentful that she had to quit. Having found something she loved doing and was extremely good at, however, she began working at it as a freelancer, and eventually got some real recognition for her work. But every time she got a great job and was on the verge of success, she would be unable to follow up or to assert herself to land the next job. She would get physically sick, or lose her momentum, or get sidetracked by a personal matter. Realizing she had done the same old thing again, she would get depressed, and then the depression would leave her without the energy, or even the will sometimes, to find enough work to pay the bills again.

It is unnerving to speak with Kelly when she is feeling defeated and is deep in her underearning. She looks like the self-assured professional she shows to the world. She's sharp, very smart, funny in a self-deprecating way, and very obviously talented at what she does. You just want to shake her and say—"Look, can't you see what I see in you?" But she can't. She cannot seem to hold on to a solid sense of herself long enough to establish a reputation and some savings she can depend on. She falls into the old self-defeating cycle because she no longer believes in herself enough to assert herself.

Underearners are always prepared for the worst, because they both fear and expect the worst. Fear of people and of economic insecurity are the basic tenets in their interaction with the world. Their expectation is that the world will respond to them as their own inner self would—"How dare you assert yourself?" They downplay their value; their unique talents and gifts are denied, or are not embraced and trusted. In this atmosphere, confusion reigns as to what talents and gifts can legitimately be claimed.

Asking for what is right and due feels nearly impossible, so underearners mostly don't receive pay commensurate with their abilities. Because they are afraid to assert themselves, they tend to deny their potential—it is recast as a case of mistaken identity.

It is impossible to escape the feeling that underearners seem divided against themselves. They fear being "found out" as a sort of guiding sensibility—as if they were pretending to be something they are not, even when they are being themselves. It is not surprising, I suppose, that survivors of abuse often become underearners and anorectic spenders.

Joan—a "bi-polar" underearner: Being an underearner does not preclude being an overspender or a debtor. In fact, many people are both. People are generally—at least for the most part—one or the other. That is why they tend to fall along lines of personality types. However, sometimes there can be swings between the two extremes, and a recovery from one can reveal the other lying in wait. Sometimes there is simply a confusing mix of virulence in both directions: extreme bravado and indulgence, mixed with underearning and anorectic spending.

Joan is that confusing kind of mix. One of the first things she ever said to me was that she was meant to lead an extraordinary life. And in many ways she has. She projects a larger-than-life presence, and she was once a trailblazer as the first woman executive at a Madison Avenue advertising agency. When she lost that job, which was an integral part of her identity, she went on a search for what to do next and wound up as a devotee in the spiritual community of a guru. Eventually she became an intimate of the guru, and a powerful presence at the center where he taught. Her life takes place in bold strokes like that. She was once even on a speaker's tour, giving a speech called "Living the Extraordinary Life."

The problem is that she is unable to live the not-so-extraordinary parts. It has been more than fifteen years since Joan lost that job at the agency. But because she cannot bring herself to take a job that is not so extraordinary, she hasn't been able to find one. She finally just gave up looking. She has worked as a temp sometimes. She has done odd jobs like painting people's apartments, or rearranging their closets. She has worked only at things that are very obviously temporary, always fostering the image that it is only a matter of time until the right fabulous situation comes along.

Primarily, she doesn't work very much at all. She has taken to living a different type of extraordinary life—a life of spending the very smallest amounts possible. Joan has also become expert at finding a certain sort of patron. She has become attached to a couple she became close with at the ashram—and they seem to like nothing better than lavishing expensive meals on her, or paying for her to take acting lessons, or flying with her to Bermuda. Joan might have a $200 dinner at the Four Seasons with her generous friends, and for the next week spend a total of eighteen dollars on the meals she pays for herself.

The paradox is that because she believes she is entitled only to meals like those at the Four Seasons, she disdains anything except those; she would rather face extreme deprivation. The fantasy of the life she thinks she should live equals an inability to accept life on life's terms. And that keeps her in a compulsive cycle of deprivation. Do we doubt that the subconscious is where genius resides? She does not buy new clothes—ever. She relies on hand-me-downs from her rich friends, because she can't possibly afford the only kind of clothes she would want to buy. She is extremely adept, when not being treated to expensive meals and expensive hand-me-downs, at employing the meal list of the anorectic spender: peanut butter and jelly, french toast, spaghetti with canned sauce, Kraft's macaroni and cheese—eaten in someone else's beautifully tailored suit.

Joan has taken to relying on the combination of periodic random jobs, the largesse of her patrons, and the ever-changing idea of a windfall making up for everything—she'll become a movie star, or an artist, or maybe hit the lottery. Meanwhile, she lives from day to day without any idea of where her next dollar is coming from.

Bob—an anorectic spender: If underearning is not defined by how much money is earned, neither is anorectic spending defined by how much money is spent. Anorectics live under a sort of siege mentality. There is a feeling of impending doom; there is certainly the guilty feeling that if even the slightest indulgence is allowed, there will be hell to pay. Anorectic spending is a painful orientation of the soul, not a quirk of the eccentric.

Bob lives alone in a basement apartment in Brooklyn. He has a job in Manhattan, to which he brings his lunch every day. He has fashioned an elaborate-sounding political reason why he doesn't take part in the office gift pool. The truth is he is mortified by the idea of actually spending five or ten dollars like that. When he is in fine form, he can buy his food for the whole week on that amount. Bob keeps his apartment cold—his father always said that was the sign of someone who came from hearty stock. Although I'm not sure anyone has ever thought that way about Bob. He looks anything but hearty.

Bob does not go out to restaurants. Neither does he go on vacation, go to the movies (sometimes he'll go to the two-dollar ones), buy new clothes (except, strangely, weird and unusual socks—which he has a collection of), have a fully furnished apartment, buy gifts for himself or for his family (except when he absolutely has to), or spend very much money on grooming. He still resents the gym membership he feels he was talked into by a pushy salesman who caught him at a weak moment.

Bob doesn't feel as if he lives in deprivation. He feels like he lives in a safe, cocoon-like world of his own manufacture. And he would never willingly choose to venture out from it. Why would he take a chance on not feeling safe? Except sometimes he gets bold enough to go on a date, or to join a discussion group at work or at the library. It is at those times that he has momentary flashes of lucidity about his living conditions. Then he feels marginal and afraid. Terrified, really.

Anorectics do not see themselves as being worth taking care of. So they try to appease the threatening gods with the extreme harnessing of desires. They also have the deep-seated suspicion that if they really let fly all their needs and desires, which they keep so neatly under wraps, they would be consumed by what they would find. They harbor the fear that they would not be able to contain them once they saw the light of day. A lot of the feeling of "safety" that anorectics feel is tied to the amount of control they feel they are able to exercise. Control is what they have. Control is what they go by.

Andrew—anorectic spending is not about modesty or being prudent: Not all anorectic spenders are as clear-cut as Bob is. Quite the contrary, most can be found only after careful examination. Some are quite rich indeed, and use anorectic spending as a way to order their world. In the extreme, careful way of anorectic control over their money, they find a way to give it meaning, by harnessing the control to reflect inner states. In the world of their anorectic spending, strict rules must be followed, or they suffer cosmic consequences that feel as real to them as if their bank balance read zero. Their deepest feelings of worthlessness are acted out before their very eyes. There is also a nice sort of dovetailing with the feeling of moral superiority compared to those who flagrantly "waste it."

Andrew has more money than he'll ever need in his lifetime. He was heir to a great fortune and has also had a nose for a profitable investment. He grew up in a very privileged material atmosphere, but in a very austere emotional one. Every luxury was at hand, but the idea of taking any pleasure from them was looked upon as indulgent and selfish in the extreme.

Andrew has fashioned a way with his money that is at once seemingly prudent, and at the same time driven by deprivation mentality. You cannot take a meal with Andrew without feeling the weight of his relationship with money. For one thing, his home is elegantly and luxuriously appointed—these trappings having been part of his inheritance. He has compartmentalized his life in many ways. For instance, in Andrew's case, there are a few areas that do not come in for extreme scrutiny or austerity. Clothes are one; he likes deeply luxurious fabrics and is partial to cashmere socks and sports coats, kid leather gloves and shoes, and coats of vicuna and alpaca.

Once those things are secured, everything else fits into his anorectic spending compartment. If his wife buys bottled water, she already knows that there will be a fight to end all fights. He has been known to walk home after a grueling medical procedure so as to save cab fare. Because there are such apparent contradictions, his friends think he is kidding them, or they implore him to stop being so ridiculous. But he doesn't think he is being the least bit ridiculous. He is quite sure it is they who are being ridiculous.

Andrew doesn't focus much attention on the effect his economizing has on his overall finances. He does not calculate the difference between what he has, and what he would have had if he weren't so economical. He has created the same sort of safe world to live in as any other anorectic. The fact that he has a fortune doesn't change his psychic response one bit. Andrew prides himself on being able to subsist on amounts of money that the lowest-earning anorectic would take pride in. Once having discovered the economy of buying rolled oats by the hundredweight, he made himself oatmeal every day for three years at a cost to him, including the sugar, of nine cents a day.

The artists: the essential conflict of underearning

I think a discussion about a few of the artists I have worked with will be illuminating to all underearners. How to earn a living while honoring their creative soul, their artistic vision, has always been the artists' essential dilemma. To a very great extent, isn't that true for a good many of us? It is certainly a struggle that underearners tend to identify with, even if they don't call themselves artists. The artist's struggle often feels like a war of truth seeking. It is not for nothing that the term "struggling artist" was coined. Most do struggle—both financially and to bring forth their deepest feelings, harnessed by their best craft. But not all artists get stuck in a compulsive cycle in which they cannot integrate their artistic vision with the practical realities of making a living.

The problem is that only one or the other seems possible, staying the course of artistic vision or taking care of the practical financial realities—but not both. It is as if they have oil, and they have vinegar, but they cannot mix them into salad dressing. The divide mirrors a certain psychic split. It sometimes seems that when an artistic vision is being followed, then that aspect of self which might be able to go out into the world and help pay the bills some other way is foreclosed upon. Likewise, if making a living becomes the dominant mode, then artistic vision can feel foreclosed on.

Finding a dignified way to earn a living while embracing and supporting the fragile part of self that is the artist is the real challenge. Debunking the myth that it is impossible is a large part of that challenge.

Dan—a living example of artistic deprivation: Dan is an accomplished artist. He is a scholar of some note and has been artist in residence at universities both here and abroad. Exhibitions of his work have garnered him awards and high praise.

Six years ago he was living in the street.

Dan fell into a period when he wasn't creating very much artwork, and thought what he was creating was terrible. He stopped showing his work to anyone. It wasn't long until he stopped creating any. Eventually, the funk paralyzed him. No longer having the feeling of renewal he got from his art, he could no longer bring himself to work at the carpentry jobs that had so happily subsidized his artwork until then. As his depression mounted, his bank account declined.

Having always earned less than his skills were worth, and less than would take care of his reasonable needs, he was used to a certain level of deprivation. Getting used to the next level, and then the next, was unfortunately easier than he had imagined. Much easier than tolerating success had ever been.

Underearners often choose to work in arenas where there is the chance for great fame and riches, a great bestowal of acceptance by the universe, but great deprivation is the quotidian norm. They live in a dream of success, but inspecting their daily lives reveals a different dream. It is never a surprise when an artist is also an underearner or anorectic. The deprivation is custom-made for the fragile, ephemeral sense of self of the artist in his creative process. And the great dream of success is a perfect front, a ruse to draw attention away from the need to make manifest a deep-seated feeling of unworthiness.

Having been raised on a farm, and steeped in the ways of small-town New England, Dan was no stranger to austerity. In fact, he found the most austere conditions the only ones tolerable sometimes. When I met him, he was living on the floors of friends' apartments. That was on good nights; bad nights were spent in the street. He felt hopeless, but almost as if he fully expected this outcome as payback for having the audacity to become an artist instead of a farmer. As if his father's harsh appraisal of him was not only correct but carried the imperative of cosmic fate. He would now be relegated to living on the streets, where he secretly felt maybe he belonged. This despite his great talent, enthusiasm, intelligence, kindness, and what to most who meet him is a deeply sensitive and caring soul.

The struggle to separate the creative and the underearning self (especially since they feel somehow to be indivisible) is a serious challenge. Many artists dwell in a place where the quality of light coming in their eastern window takes on far greater importance than the balance in the checkbook. Sometimes that is as it should be; sometimes it is a device used to deflect attention away from chronic underearning.

Sarah—a sensitive soul: If you were to meet Sarah, you would not mistake her for an advertising executive or Wall Street worker. At first sight, it is hard to imagine anything except that she is an artist. You can sense it in the way she walks down the street. You can feel an otherworldliness, an ethereal glow about her. She spends a lot of time on what can only be described as another plane.

I have never met a more sensitive soul. Ever since she was a very young girl, Sarah knew she wanted to be an artist. There was no denying her gift—teachers began sending notes home to her parents as early as the third grade, describing her talent as a rare thing. She wasn't like the other kids, but that didn't feel like a hardship to her, since she never really understood why anyone would want to be like the other kids anyway.

Sarah is a little bit fragile when it comes to making her way in the practical world. She certainly never became adept at handling money—nor for that matter did she give that much thought to earning it or how to use it to take care of herself. It may even be that she never really regarded money as something absolutely necessary in life. She immersed herself in the study of her art and in the inner world of her art. She studied with accomplished and caring teachers and she became accomplished in her own right.

Once she had completed her advanced studies, she found a subsidized live/work loft and was ready to start her career. But the subsidy didn't include a stipend of any sort and she had no income and no real plan. There was no money for food or even for paint—and she was really scared for the first time. Huge chunks of reality began crowding in. She went to a temp agency so she could earn some money somehow, and was assigned to filing jobs because she had not learned to type. Although her needs were modest, living in New York on the wages from file temping is a constant trial. She began to despair that her life up until then had been a fairy tale, and that this harsh life of filing and learning to type and filling in as the girl from the temp agency was what she was really destined for, what she really deserved. The long hours of mind-numbing work and the long hours of worry about money drained her energy and the passion for her art.

The following ten years were really a struggle to keep her art light burning while keeping the bill collectors from the door. The spiral of shame and self-doubt that began with that first temp job did not go away. It seemed to her as though her existence as an artist in training, which felt so sheltered and charmed, was actually only a cruel hoax. As though she must have known somewhere all along that it was foolish to think she deserved such a life. Debts grew. Pressures grew. Her marriage to a like-minded artist saw its own difficult dynamics take shape. He wasn't much better at this money thing than she was.

Sarah desperately wanted her life back. She wondered where things had gone so terribly wrong. When I met her she couldn't figure out how to make any time at all for her artwork. She was struggling with how to pay all her bills on time. She definitely didn't know what to do about the debt she had built up or how to handle the fact that bill collectors were now threatening her. She was a wreck.

The challenge of integrating an artistic vision with the practical realities of earning a living can be daunting—but they are by no means mutually exclusive. Despite the complications of separating what are simply the trials of being an artist, from what are parts of the addictive cycle that need to be broken, the same prescription for healing works for the artist/underearner.

British psychoanalyst D. W. Winnicott said, "Through artistic expression we can hope to keep in touch with our primitive selves whence the most intense feelings and even fearfully acute sensations derive, and we are poor indeed if we are only sane."

Money and Couples

All couples have conflicts about money. When money disorders figure in the equation, however, things tend to get complicated fast, and the atmosphere can become thick with resentment. Money disorders amplify and distort the natural tension in a couple. Accusations are made, feelings get hurt, resentments are buried deep under a tide of blame placing, the blueprint for which is learned early on in our families. Feelings and expectations about money run deep. It is by no means as simple as this, but here goes—however much we may bridle at the thought, most people tend to become either very much like, or very much the opposite of, one of their parents in their money roles. For that matter it isn't all that unheard of for them to marry the other one.

In couples with money disorders, the adage about the rocks in his head fitting perfectly into the holes in her head is usually apt. Opposites attract. It is a rare thing to find a couple one of whose halves has a clear-cut money disorder and the other is perfectly healthy in relationship to money. He says, "I'd be all right if she would just stop nagging." She says, "I'd stop nagging, if he'd stop spending." Feelings intensify when they are attached to money, and then are acted out within the couple. By the time most couples seek help, the anger and resentment on each side is fairly well established, and their patterns have usually become deeply ingrained.

A particular brand of codependency develops in couples with money disorders. The efforts to control, and the inordinate involvement with someone else's finances, are basically similar to any codependent situation. They turn the focus away from one's own life and onto the couple. Sometimes it is hard to tease out what are the practical realities of running a household from a codependent money disorder cycle. The fact that whatever dynamics are being expressed requires both partners, gets denied. Codependent money disorders are usually part of a package deal in any case; other symptoms are present but obscured by the focus on the other partner.

The prescription for a couple in an obsessive money cycle is for each partner to work out his or her own money problems before tackling problems as a couple. It is imperative that each individual be clear about his needs, goals, and expectations. A couple can't work toward common goals until each partner is on solid ground. Often the individual's needs are obscured in the constant vying back and forth for power within the couple. When things are working optimally, I imagine a couple as being like two trees, each strongly rooted in the ground and choosing freely to mingle their branches. Not like trees needing to lean against each other for support, they are self-contained, able to choose without feeling desperate.

Christine and Mathew—opposites attract: One example so common as to be a cliché is the introverted or codependent woman with a tendency toward underearning or anorectic spending hooking up with an indulgent man whose spending and debting is out of control. In the best of all worlds, one would complement the other. By the time I see a couple, however, the complementary traits that were so appealing have transformed themselves into polarized and fortified camps. It is easy to imagine what transpires.

I recently met with Christine and Mathew, a couple engaged to be married. They have been together four years and living together for two. They have fallen into a pattern that troubles Christine, so much so that she has put the wedding on hold. She has always kept a low profile and has been a consistent underearner, but had no debt until she moved in with Mathew. Since they've been living together, Christine and Mathew's credit card debt has grown to $32,000 and counting.

Since Mathew has always had credit problems, Christine got the credit cards in her name, so the debts are now legally her responsibility, and she feels suffocated beneath them. She was originally glad to help out by using her unblemished credit rating, but her discomfort while watching the debt grow has now turned into something more like rage. Mathew's promises to stop incurring any more debt, sincere when he makes them, especially in the face of Christine's tears, never last very long. He cannot stop spending. When a newer, cooler computer comes out—he has to buy it. I don't mean wants to buy it—I mean *has* to buy it. Keep their four-year-old Honda? There was no way. Trying to stop Mathew from buying a new Explorer this year would have been about as fruitful as trying to stop a crowd from gathering in Times Square on New Year's Eve. To Mathew, $72 Sunday green fees, and $48 cashmere socks feel like inalienable rights. After all, he says, doesn't he deserve a little pleasure after working all week?

And Christine agrees; she wants nothing more than for Mathew to be happy; in fact, she positions her whole life around trying to make him happy, almost as if her own happiness should be considered only as an afterthought. Except she never really bargained for all the debt. Her father was irresponsible with money and this whole scenario feels terribly familiar to her, a completely unwanted *déjà vu*. She is profoundly confused at how she wound up in this position, so she tries desperately to control Mathew's spending. She puts him on budgets.

She allocates only a specific amount of cash to him for the week. She tells him how much it scares her to be in debt. As I'm sure you've guessed, nothing works.

Actually, Mathew feels as if Christine is the culprit. She's always controlling him, he says. "Christine has me on a budget again," he complains to his buddies by way of explaining that he can't go out with them that night. "Yes, sweetheart. I'm taking my lunch to work and I won't go out for a drink afterward. No, I won't go buy any more DVDs." But after a while of submitting like that, he starts to feel as if he's in a pressure cooker, as if his friends think he's a wimp, and if he doesn't let out some of the steam soon, he'll explode. At that point, he doesn't buy a new DVD—he buys a whole new wardrobe, or a sleek new titanium bike. Mathew has the idea that, really, all he needs to do is pay down his debt with his bonus at the end of the year. And he did exactly that last year: he used his bonus to pay down a significant amount of debt. But only six months later the debt was higher than ever before. He complains that Christine doesn't think big, and that her small thinking holds him back. "Sometimes I get stuck in there with her negativity. And then I can't do my thing. But later I feel like she's right—I do spend too much, and then I feel guilty." And so it goes.

The atmosphere is suffused with expected roles, with dashed dreams. When couples come together, they bring along a constellation of subconscious desires and expectations, all their emotional freight, and all their history. Christine always thought that when she got married, her husband would earn more than she did, and would help her bridge the gap between her low earnings and what she hoped for herself. Although she never felt quite worthy of living an abundant life, maybe her husband's coattails could help hide her terrible feelings of inadequacy. She feels as if their debt might have been some kind of cosmic price exacted, consistent with all her darkest doubts about herself. For his part, Mathew always thought he would be the kind of provider Christine imagined, and in his heart he believes he is. Mathew sees himself as a high-flyer who hasn't quite reached his cruising altitude yet. He understands what Christine is afraid of, and he is more than compliant about working on it together, but if Christine wasn't pressing the matter and deferring the wedding plans, Mathew would probably not describe their situation as all that problematic.

What's really going on? Christine earns far less than her ability and education would suggest, and she is an anorectic spender. She likes to keep her life safe and small. That doesn't mean there isn't a side of her longing to expand and take risks. There is. It's just that it only gets expressed through Mathew. Mathew, on the other hand, is a gregarious salesman, a compulsive spender and debtor, who likes to live on the edge, pushing himself, spending and enjoying with abandon, worrying about consequences later. But neither does that mean he doesn't have a side that wants to be more prudent, to create a stable life. Somehow Mathew wants what Christine has, and Christine wants what Mathew has, though maybe neither wants quite so much as the other has. If the subconscious drive is to hook up with someone who will provide the complementary traits we are missing and produce balance—that's not what usually happens.

What happens is more prosaic; the two types clash. They become *more* like they were—not less. What they do is rail against each other. They blame each other for everything that's wrong. Which doesn't mean it's a bad match. In fact, things can be full of hope, if they can move the focus to where it belongs. When a couple breaks an addictive money cycle, what were once seen as liabilities become assets. Then the sought after balance can finally occur.

In Christine's case, she is afraid to talk about money in a clear and comprehensive way, to discuss what she earns versus what Mathew earns and to decide what percentage of expenses they are each going to pay. She is terrified of asserting her needs and of revealing how inadequate her earnings feel to her. She is also extremely loath to provoke Mathew, for she knows that any discussion that might seem designed to deprive him of the toys he craves is destined for acrimony. And she isn't exactly the model of self-confidence in the relationship area, even where money is not the issue.

Different incomes; difficult feelings

This is a very common problem for couples. Most couples earn somewhat different amounts of money. And all couples have strong feelings about that. Sometimes the variance is small, such as one partner earning 55 percent and the other 45 percent but sometimes it's more like one earning 90 percent and the other 10 percent. The proportions are truly irrelevant; there are always going to be lots of feelings about how much each partner earns and about how that money is spent, even where the partners have exact parity of income. If there has never been a wide-ranging discussion about what each partner needs and expects, there is a pretty good chance that a lot of feelings won't be aired. Even when these conversations do take place, it is difficult at best to coax the real feelings out of hiding; the power struggles often mask fears that may not want to see the light of day.

A new struggle for couples and money has been happening a lot lately. Women who came of age placing equal weight on career and marriage and family suddenly have discovered their visceral feelings collide with their principle of parity in relationships and in earning power. Many such women have told me they were not prepared for the flood of feelings about family and children they felt once they were married. Ancient blueprints, which they thought they had eschewed, came rushing in—unbidden. All of a sudden, that old, dismissed idea that their husbands should take care of them becomes hard to shake. They may never admit it out loud, perhaps not even to themselves, but there it is. Now what?

There is another wrinkle on the traditional couple roles when a postfeminist woman has a powerful opposite response to a similar feeling. I've spoken to many women who can't understand how, having rejected the traditional roles, they adopt them in reverse. These women, married to men who become dependent on them in the classic style, find themselves taking on the role of caretaker and breadwinner in the family. A lot of the pent-up and unspoken content of these relationships is attached to money—and a sort of holy war develops about who will win.

A disparity of income: I saw a couple a few years ago made up of one partner earning 95 percent of the income and another earning only 5 percent. It was certainly in the nature of their work—Annie is a music teacher and part-time musician, and Daniel is an investment banker—that there would be a great disparity in their incomes. When they moved in together, Daniel naturally wanted to live in a grander apartment than Annie could afford. "Fair enough that I should be the one to pay for it, then," he said, and offered to pay most of the rent. As time went on, however, Daniel's largesse began to gnaw at him whenever they did anything that cost real money. Annie couldn't keep up, Daniel had to pay, and Daniel was silently resentful. Annie struggled, too. She struggled with how not being able to pay made her feel like a failure, and with how it underscored the sacrifices of her lifestyle rather than the benefits. Mostly what happened was that Daniel simply paid, and said nothing—but couples know when something is up, and when there is something the couple avoids talking about—nothing much else gets talked about either.

"Why don't you get a real job that pays real money?" was what Daniel finally said. "I didn't know that I was going to have to foot the bills for you forever. And besides, it's like you're wasting your life. Like you're living a pipe dream of hitting it big on Broadway. And I'm the Sugar Daddy expected to finance the whole shebang." Annie was dumbfounded. She thought they had an understanding. It wasn't easy for her either. "I thought I had made it clear that I don't earn anywhere near as much as you, and probably never will, but I thought you were all right with that."

Annie is an underearner and struggles with her creative identity.

She has been the musical director for many off-Broadway musicals. She has played the piano in prestigious concerts. As with many creative people, sometimes her confidence fails her and she falls into deep doubt and depression. At those times she stops showing up for herself, and in fear, settles for whatever menial jobs are on offer. That's when the hopelessness sets in, and she starts to feel baffled about why everything eventually goes so wrong. Like clockwork, when Annie goes into a funk, Daniel goes into overdrive. He dives even further into his manic workaholic cycle. Daniel thinks nothing of working the night through, then changing into a clean shirt, never having considered going home. He apparently has a positive genius for a particular type of corporate deal making and is held in very high regard at his firm. His bonus last year was almost as much as Annie has made in her lifetime.

Daniel eventually came clean that his resentment wasn't all about Annie. Once, he had abandoned his own dream of leading a creative life, a dream that began when he was still in college. It turns out that he once saw himself as a writer with legitimate promise. And now Annie was acting out, right in front of his eyes, his worst nightmare—to choose a life that sounds down to a very deep emotional place but is an abject failure financially. Just what he so elaborately defended against in his own life. All the accusations hurled at Annie during this period he now sees were actually meant for that side of himself that was still trying to find expression.

The shared expenses: working out the feelings

In breaking an obsessive cycle, one big issue that brings forth all manner of underlying feelings is how to handle what each partner will contribute toward expenses. And a big part of that issue is how to separate out all those feelings in order to make rational decisions, and to get the resentments and the past out of the decision making process. Dealing with disproportionate earnings is always a challenge. It doesn't really matter whether you are the lower or the higher earning partner, both have their own brand of fear. The higher earner might feel taken advantage of, or harbor the deeper fear of only being worthy of love by virtue of money. The lower earner may feel guilty, inadequate, or privately resentful about not pulling equal weight. He fears that his dreams and desires will get short shrift, or that they won't be honored equally. And very often the more acquiescent partner's dreams *are* relegated to the back burner.

Should expenses be shared fifty-fifty regardless of income? Should couples keep their money separate and only contribute to expenses that are communal, keeping all personal expenses separate? If so, should the communal expenses be shared fifty-fifty, or in proportion to earnings?

In my own life, my wife and I have always kept our finances separate. We contribute equally to the shared expenses such as rent, utilities, and groceries equally, and keep the personal spending separate. There have been periods in our marriage, however, when I have not brought in as much income as Elizabeth. At those times, Elizabeth agreed to pay a larger portion of our expenses than her usual 50 percent. There were also times when I brought in the larger share of money and I paid more than my 50 percent. I don't want to give the impression that these decisions came without any ambivalence or that we didn't have strong feelings about it—she did, and I did.

We have never been a very traditional couple in our marital roles; I certainly don't think anyone has ever accused me of being macho or Elizabeth of being a shrinking violet. For instance, I do the grocery shopping, the cooking, and a lot of the housework. Elizabeth reminds me when the cereal she likes is low by leaving the box on the kitchen counter when it's empty. She doesn't quite seem to capture the idea of not leaving muffin crumbs behind on the counter. And we like it that way. Nonetheless, it has never been easy to accept my role, untraditional as it may be, as someone who has to rely on his wife to pay more than her share of the bills—even temporarily. But after processing our feelings, so as not to be sideswiped by them during the planning process, we made a new financial plan for that time period. Similarly, when I was in the higher earning position, Elizabeth struggled with seeing herself as a more traditional wife who relies on her husband's income.

Cindy and Darren, stuck in the numbers: Eventually it doesn't matter exactly what the couple's dynamics are—recovery will always follow the same few steps. Each member needs to do recovery work before the couple comes together to work things out. I do not mean to suggest that both members of a couple need to seek help in order for one partner to begin recovery. Frankly, one member can recover quite nicely even if the other member has no interest in changing. It is admittedly harder that way, but by no means impossible. At the very least, getting some personal clarity, and stopping whatever individual addictive cycle there is, will go a long way toward clearing up confusion about dynamics within the couple.

I recently worked with a couple who were as stuck as stuck could be in their anger and resentment toward each other, and their fights about money were more or less constant. After working with each of them individually and establishing Spending Plans that took care of their needs, I brought them together to address their issues as a couple. Many things were aired about each partner's feelings regarding decisions about money, and about whether the hopes, and dreams, and desires of each were honored equally. Both wanted to be clear about who spends how much on what. Darren was earning approximately 74 percent of the couple's income, with Cindy earning 26 percent. They had never discussed it, but they sure had lots of thoughts and feelings about it. Now that they each had worked out a plan, it was time to decide whether they were going to keep their money separate, mingle the money, or keep it separate for individual expenses and joint for joint expenses.

Darren and Cindy chose to keep their money separate for a while to see how that worked for each of them. They decided, however, to com-

bine their money when it came to shared expenses such as the mortgage, utilities, insurance, cable, groceries, etc. We discussed the options:
because Darren is earning so much more he could simply pay the
shared expenses, or they could each pay 50 percent, or they could contribute according to their respective percentage of earnings. They
decided on the percentage of earning plan. And they were visibly
relieved.

Darren and Cindy could have initially decided to pool their funds
instead of keeping them separate. That would not be antithetical to
each keeping a Spending Plan. What would have happened is that
each Spending Plan would have been incorporated into a master
Spending Plan for the couple, which is simply a joining of the two. It
doesn't matter which way a couple chooses—it only matters that
everything is made clear and brought into the open in an honest
exchange.

Money, Therapy, and Depression

The problem with psychotherapy for people with money disorders is that it can be uncommonly frustrating—for both the patient and the therapist. Beside the money or work obsession, people with money disorders exhibit mostly the same symptoms others generally seek therapy for: fear, anxiety, problems with relationships, feelings of alienation, a lack of integrity or integration. Relief is sought from psychic or psychosomatic pain. Initially, those with money disorders may find the process of talking in therapy comforting and helpful. But over time, the psychotherapeutic process fails.

What happens is that fears and complaints about money take center stage at each therapy session. The obsessive worry about money or work is unrelenting. If the therapist doesn't have a practical or quick solution to offer for the money or work problems, the patient considers the therapeutic enterprise to be a colossal waste of time. Eventually, as the therapist fails to offer practical solutions, the dam finally breaks. "I don't care where this came from or why I do it—I need help now. I can't even pay your bill." Any attempt by the therapist to draw the focus of the interaction back to the underlying emotional terrain is met with more roadblocks than a military installation.

This might sound like any typical resistance in therapy. But it is not. Most resistance is just resistance, and overcoming it is an integral part of the work. Patients and therapists alike get confused because struggles with work, money, relationships, and meaning are the very stuff of therapy to begin with. But here they are symptoms, first and foremost, of a money disorder, and not just an expression of existential conflict. Until the nuts and bolts of money disorders are addressed, this material functions as a distracting smokescreen. Therapy with money addicts, therefore, is like that for any addict—without addressing the addiction directly, the therapy hasn't got much of a chance. Hoping a money disorder will simply dissipate after the patient gains enough insight is exactly like hoping an alcoholic will simply stop drinking after he gains enough insight. As we all know, that is not how it works.

Eventually, the therapy devolves into a more or less constant struggle between the patients' urgent demands for solutions to their money problems, and the therapists' wish to get to deeper causes. None of the therapists' most trusted techniques seem to work, and many of their most piercing insights don't get through. Therefore, people with money disorders may be viewed as concrete, or as help-rejecting complainers. But until the addictive money cycle gets broken progress in therapy may be impossible.

Sometimes a therapist finds him- or herself on the horns of a dilemma. The patient complains about the fee and intimates that the therapist is adding to money pressures by demanding such a large amount for therapy. The therapist commiserates and, believing the patient profoundly needs the therapy, lets the patient run up a bill. The patient may develop a mirror image of the therapist's belief: the self-reinforcing fear that he desperately needs the therapy but can't afford it. This combination does not work out very well. Once a therapist effectively loans money to the patient, he or she has unwittingly set up a no-win situation.

I have been on the receiving end of complaints about impasses such as these from both sides. Patients have described the pervasive feeling of pressure from the debt owed to the therapist. I have also listened to the confusion and resentment therapists can feel toward patients who owe them money.

These dynamics compound therapists' ambivalence toward the commercial aspects of being a helping professional. In fact, therapists exhibit a particular brand of underearning suffused with moral conflict, capped by the belief that perhaps they shouldn't be paid at all. Even therapists who don't have their own difficulties with money often have difficulty engaging in a frank discussion about the practical realities of money.

I remember a certain therapist whose patient owed her $40,000. I asked why she let the debt get so big. She told me about her attachment to this woman, who had fought a lifelong battle with depression, and with whom she had been working for several years before she extended credit. She believed that the patient truly needed her help, and that she would feel extremely guilty if she stopped seeing her because of money. I asked her why she hadn't seen the patient for a fee the patient could afford, or if she felt so strongly about it, for no fee at all. For that matter, notwithstanding the strong bond and working alliance between patient and therapist, why hadn't she considered making a referral to a clinic or other provider early on—before the situation got so bad? In the end, the therapy disintegrated into a morass of stickiness and blame about money and dependency.

This was a very unusual situation, for I later got to see the patient. She said that a great deal of her time was spent worrying about the debt to her therapist. She also told me about how she desperately tried to "get better faster" so she wouldn't have to owe so much money. She felt ashamed at what her therapist must think of her. Not being able to pay confirmed her worst fears about herself and her feelings of worthlessness.

Extreme examples abound. I remember a woman who continually tried to end her therapy, but her therapist would not allow it. He kept insisting that he would lower his fee, and that he would let her run a bill. Despite her telling him of her continued uneasiness about that arrangement, he continued to insist.

The feelings stirred up on both sides can be fertile ground for therapist and patient. But they can get lost in that ground. Often the therapist becomes overinvolved, believes herself to be irreplaceable, and loses the ability to give the patient her evenly suspended attention. The patient, for her part, loses the ability to think about anything except the money she owes the therapist, and feels that this is yet another horrible example of how she is hopelessly imprisoned by her chronic money troubles.

Depression and money disorders: which came first?

Depression can often be found in lockstep with money disorders. It is never easy to tease out which came first: did a depressive episode trigger an intense addictive response, or did the addiction beget the depression? I'm not convinced it would be all that instructive to learn the answer. The difficulty is similar to distinguishing whether a psychosomatic symptom came first, or the fear attendant with it actually caused the symptom in the first place. Suffice it to say that they come in pairs. The divide in the psyche/soma is as permeable and fluid as the financial/emotional divide in money disorders. Not surprisingly, many people with money disorders also have psychosomatic syndromes.

The great problem with depression and money disorders is that they form not only a pair but a perfect symbiotic relationship. They feed off each other, and make it much more difficult to treat either one. "How in the world will I ever be able to overcome my money problems, when I'm so prone to falling into bouts of debilitating depression" is what I hear from so many sufferers. "And my money problems are the biggest part of why I get depressed." Even when the depression is not debilitating, the feelings of hopelessness are more or less the same, and the idea of putting one's finances straight while battling what feels like a vortex of despair seems an impossibility, beyond the pale. And it does feel impossible—but is not. When the addictive cycle is broken first, and a supportable structure is put in its place, then whatever traction had been missing from therapy can finally be established.

I remember a man who had begun his recovery from his money disorder and was back in therapy. He told his therapist that he was committed to living his life on a cash basis and therefore had to pay at the end of each session. The therapist said that would be fine but continued to offer the standard arrangement of sending him a bill at the end of the month. During the course of the therapy, the therapist maintained that he was happy to receive a hundred-dollar bill after each session. But he revealed that the money was very much on his mind when he asked the patient to imagine with him a hypothetical he had envisioned: A man and therapist meet for a number of years, three times a week. During the therapy they delve deep into all manner of psychic material, and find their way through all type of conflict and transference. "Here's the thing," he posited. "What if everything else they did was only done for the sake of that instant when the money passed from one hand to the other? What if that was the only moment carrying all the meaning?"

When a money disorder takes center stage in therapy, then the moments carrying all the meaning *will* be the moments about money—both inside and outside the therapist's office. Unfortunately, by that point, achieving any real traction in the therapy may have become impossible, unless the compulsive cycle is broken.

Money and the Recovering Addict

Money is particularly troublesome for people in recovery. Addicts of all stripes often continue to have stubbornly entrenched money problems long into their recovery from other addictions. I know of no surer route to depression and despair for a recovering addict than chronic and baffling trouble with money. I regularly field calls from people with five, ten, twenty-five years of recovery who are at their wit's end about money and work. And it's not just the bill collectors who are typically demanding reparations; their intimate relationships bear the brunt as well. Despite profound changes in most areas of their lives, addictive money problems continue to occupy a fortified position.

The phenomenon of switching addictions is well known, of course. Addiction has been likened to a ten-headed dragon: once you think you've cut its head off, another head pops up for you to do battle with. It is my experience that one of the dragon's heads is money addiction. Recovering alcoholics and substance abusers often become addicted to money and work. Deep money trouble may have been a problem their whole lives, but often it has been obscured, or at least put on the back burner for a while, during recovery from other addictions. After all, not only do addictions switch but they also coexist, and different ones ascend at different times. When one round of the battle seems to be won, the dragon says, "Here, you forgot about this—deal with this." Money is a perfect medium for exposing the twin edges of the proverbial sword of addiction: grandiosity paired with low self-esteem.

Kevin, the perfect example: Kevin is a perfect example of grandiosity/low self-esteem. He lives in a lavishly furnished, million-dollar apartment on Central Park West. He probably has forty suits, and maybe a hundred shirts, but is rarely able to pay the rent on time. The landlord gets his full attention only after the marshal has attached an eviction notice to his door.

Kevin struggles with one of the primary bugaboos of the addict—entitlement. He feels entitled to a life of luxury and recognition. It is not that he doesn't have prodigious talent; he does. A talented architect, he has watched his own star rise more than once. The problem for Kevin lies in the periods when he is not making the big money and receiving the big praise. He has fashioned a lifestyle for himself based on his highest earning days and can't bear the ego bruise involved with adjusting it downward during leaner times.

Trying to keep up with a very well-heeled crowd, Kevin has pushed every credit card he could get his hands on to their very substantial limits. He owes everyone he knows: his brother, his sister, his best friend, even his ex-wife, from whom he managed a loan. His creditors have taken up permanent residence on his voice mail. Frightened and ashamed, and with no more Peters left to borrow from to pay all the Pauls, Kevin finally called me. Sober for twenty years, this money thing, he had to finally admit, had him beat.

Just that day, Kevin had put a $3,000 suit on hold at Armani. Sometimes it is hard to remember, when faced with bravado and bluster, entitlement and posturing, that they are symptoms of feelings of worthlessness, not the reverse.

Robert: a different insight: Robert's story is different. Also in recovery from alcoholism for a long time, his life revolves around his recovery; his dedication and service to it is unquestioned. What he can't understand is why getting money straight in his life has been the one thing that remains elusive.

Robert is a pillar of the recovering community where he lives. Hundreds of people come to seek his counsel and his kind encouragement. He is probably an example of giving until it hurts. His commitment to helping people through the trials of their recovery is complete. Robert gives so much of his time, and so much of his energy, that his own needs often go begging.

Robert's business is more often than not in a cash crisis. Subscribing to the prevailing twelve-step philosophy, Robert believes his problems with money will work themselves out over time. And for some people, that is what happens. A lot of recovering addicts see their money troubles dissipate during their time in recovery. But not those with money disorders. In fact, for Robert, things have gotten dramatically worse over time. Now he has come face-to-face with the very real prospect of losing his business.

Robert has been a recovering alcoholic for twenty-seven years. During that time he has stopped taking drugs, addressed his long-time compulsive overeating, quit smoking, and quit drinking coffee. He is still dabbling with abstaining from sugar and white flour as well. But just like so many before him, the last thing he was willing to face were his chronic problems with money.

Money: a substance like any other

Most addicts have a money disorder of one form or another. Recovering cocaine addicts tend to be compulsive spenders and debtors, marijuana addicts often get stuck in ruts of unrealized potential, anorectic eaters tend to have anorectic spending disorders, and so on. There is a very substantial coaddiction among all the process addictions; particularly intertwined are food, money, and relationship addictions.

Chronic money problems exist on a continuum, however, and are a matter of degree. For some, they never become critical or painful enough to drive them to seek help. For others, the problems dissipate over the course of their recovery. For still others, however, money problems become deeply impacted, and the confusion and despair they cause may be the most painful and protracted difficulties in their lives.

Amy does everything she can to enhance her recovery. She is in group psychotherapy, she studies yoga, she is devoted to vitamin and herb therapies, and you might call her more than a little bit of a stickler about her health-food regimens. She is a survivor of abuse, she comes from an alcoholic home, and she has struggled with her co-dependency for as long as she can remember.

At the intersection of all these issues lies money. Because she's convinced that there won't be enough for her, Amy tries with a super-human effort to earn money. She is more or less always in a state of fatigue. She is afraid she will be "found out" as the fraud she still believes she is. Every time she resolves to really get a handle on "this money thing," she inevitably goes into a fog; she loses her checkbook, she forgets about ATM withdrawals and starts bouncing checks, she misses meetings and sabotages her work.

Powered by fear and doubt, and in perpetual motion, Amy has enough energy for six jobs. But she can't seem to harness the energy on her own behalf. She doesn't apply for jobs that she is suited for and perfectly capable of, based on her fear of being found out. She is expert at figuring out everything that will go wrong in any promising situation, thereby obviating any need to actually try it. Amy has brought all her intelligence and energy to bear, but this last addiction just won't budge.

Amy isn't alone. "Why haven't my money problems gotten any better during my recovery?" "I can't deal with all this money stuff anymore—twenty-one years of sobriety and nothing seems to have changed." "I'm a lawyer, for God's sake, why am I always in debt?" I hear it every day. "I have a Ph.D. from an Ivy League school, why am I working for peanuts?" "I've tried, I just can't stop spending."

Even Bill W. continued to struggle with money in recovery

I get a lot of these calls. All of these people have been vigilant about their recovery; that is not the problem. The fact is that identifying money addictions, or money disorders, is a far newer phenomenon than with most other addictions. It is also among the last to have a very real stigma attached. In a world where accomplishments are measured more and more in dollars and cents, an admission that money is out of control in your life is viewed as an admission of failure. Compounding the shame, this attitude toward money penetrates the usually nonjudgmental rooms of AA. Men are especially loath to admit their money problems, often equating their value as men with their value as earners and achievers. The promise that "fear of economic insecurity will leave us" never comes to pass for someone stuck in an addictive money cycle.

Another factor that keeps money disorders in the shadows is the notion that trusting a higher power is fine, but when it comes to money—well, that's a different story. "Yeah, I trust in a higher power. But I'm sure as hell not going to give over my trust when it comes to my money." It is well known, of course, that even Bill Wilson, the founder of Alcoholics Anonymous, continued to be plagued by money worries throughout his recovery. The willfulness attached to money and work can be stubborn indeed. Blind spots, sacred cows, and sheer unadulterated will all conspire to do their worst.

Bob's willfulness: Bob is a divorced single parent of a nine-year-old girl. He has been in recovery from alcoholism and drug abuse for four years. When he said that he earned $36,000 a year but that he owed $48,000 I asked him a few questions about his expenses. They did not seem out of proportion to his earnings, and I didn't understand the genesis of his current crisis. I asked him to tell me more, and, in passing, he mentioned his daughter's private school. "Private school? Your daughter's in private school? You never mentioned that in all our discussions of your expenses. How much is the tuition?" Without blinking an eye, Bob replied, "Twenty-one thousand dollars."

"I guess we may want to take a look at that, huh?" I said. To which he replied, "That is the one category I am not willing to change." So I put it to him: "But without changing that, how will you break the cycle of debt you're in?" He told me, "I think I can get my eating expenses down as low as nine dollars a week. I can do stuff like that." But Bob is blind to to the insanity of his plan. He literally believes that taking his lunch to work and giving up new clothes will offset the $21,000 in tuition—fully 60 percent of his take-home pay. Extreme economizing, even if it *could* offset the tuition, would reinforce rather than break his addictive cycle, unless he establishes a balanced plan to take care of his needs.

Money disorders: the last stronghold of addiction

Many recovering addicts report that getting over their money disorders was considerably harder than dealing with their other addictions. Of course, whatever the next addiction, it always feels like the hardest to deal with because the path gets narrower. Still, the abject fear that there is not enough is the taproot feeling of addiction. And feelings about money aren't new—they go way down deep and way back when. It is not surprising, then, that going down as deep as they do, they last as long as they do.

A certain spiritual pride also does its worst in keeping recovering addicts from dealing with their money disorder. The prospect of becoming a beginner again can be both daunting and humiliating. Paradoxically, the more solid the recovery in other areas, the more difficult it can be to begin anew. Who wants to feel humbled again? But if the goal of recovery from addiction is to feel feelings instead of acting them out, and to have an unfettered and expansive life—then addictive money patterns must be broken to enjoy a full recovery.

Addictive money disorders siphon off the joy from recovery.

Deeply entrenched money disorders are high on the list of predictive factors for relapse. Relapse, however, is not the most common result: that is frustration and fear, depression and hopelessness. Struggling with a money disorder is no fun. Feelings of doom can insert themselves into what is probably a less than solid sense of self in any case for most addicts. After all, they think, "Aren't smart people like me supposed to be able to handle stuff like this without jumping the tracks?"

Recovering addicts try myriad ways to deal with their money problems. Psychotherapy is often sought—but insight alone does not break an addictive money cycle. Debt consolidation and consumer credit agencies are another avenue—but debt consolidation is to a money disorder as methadone maintenance is to heroin addiction. It puts a Band-Aid on but does nothing to get to root causes and conditions.

Debtors Anonymous is the twelve-step recovery program designed specifically to help people with money addictions. Recovering addicts resist Debtors Anonymous more than other twelve-step programs— with all their might. There are certainly wholesale miracles to be witnessed at DA in the turnarounds in people's lives, and I can't recommend it highly enough—but DA continues to be a hard sell. People complain that the cohesiveness of more established programs like Alcoholics Anonymous seems to be missing, while also pointing out that it is hard to tune out the high noise-to-signal ratio in order to hear the real message.

Addictions counselors have adopted a position over the years similar to the one proffered in twelve-step recovery rooms—that if you are vigilant enough in your recovery, then your money difficulties will work themselves out eventually. I don't want to repeat myself *ad infinitum*—but it does not work that way for those with a money disorder. What happens is the reverse: the money disorder progresses until the recovery from other addictions is threatened.

The essential recovery goals of reducing arrogance and grandiosity, while raising self-esteem, remain elusive while the recovering addict still has an active money disorder. I can't think of anything more at cross-purposes with recovery. If anything, money disorders raise arrogance and grandiosity while lowering self-esteem.

I am happy to report that more and more addictions counselors have become sensitive to the dramatic effect an untreated money disorder can have in a recovering addict's life. Counselors have become aware that no matter how diligently addicts or alcoholics work their program, a money disorder can cause them to jump the tracks. There are now quite a few counselors who specialize in treating money disorders. Any treatment plan—and especially any relapse prevention plan—is incomplete without an assessment of money disorders and incorporation of their treatment into the recovery plan.

Clarity

Clarity is the main weapon in the fight against the most pervasive and perhaps the most pernicious problem for those with money disorders: vagueness. Establishing clarity and coming out from behind the shroud of vagueness is the point of departure into recovery. In this chapter, I'm going to describe a group of what I call "clarity tools." These are the practical steps to take to bring an end to the self-defeating patterns of a money disorder.

When we talk about money, it is never just about money. So many feelings compete for attention; their urgent demands are clearly *felt*, perhaps not so clearly *understood*. We load a ton of emotional freight onto money's back; expectations and desires are transferred to it, unresolved conflict and family history are attached to it. Obsessive money cycles are custom made for individual personalities. They ingeniously accomplish their misdirection—while producing an obsession with money or work so compelling that it keeps the focus off what really matters.

Think of your money disorder as having its own personality some-where inside of you. The first thing I can tell you with some degree of confidence is this: it does not want to relinquish control. The second thing is that it will come up with more and more ingenious ways to hijack your psyche, newer and better symptoms to keep you occupied. Just because you decide to break the cycle doesn't mean it will cooperate. Everyone's resistance to breaking a money cycle is different. But there is always resistance. Some experience it as not particularly formidable; once given the tools for recovery they seem to be off and running. Others meet resistance at every turn, and they can't seem to get on track. Once they do, it takes great vigilance, discipline, and tons of support to keep them there. Most people fall somewhere in the middle, needing at least a moderate amount of support to stay the course.

Why is support so important? Frankly, the principles and tools of recovery can be grasped pretty easily by the average sixth grader. They are deceptively simple; they are simple, but they are not easy. Old patterns die hard. And old money patterns are particularly hard to break, because there is so much emotional material attached to them. Anger and grandiosity take their best shot: "Why should I have to do all this?" "Don't you know who I am?" Fear and low self-esteem chime in as well: "I don't deserve anything." "Just who do I think I am?" If the emotional and the financial realms didn't intersect in this way, then the advice of financial advisers and well-meaning friends would work like a charm. But the emotional *does* intersect with the financial. Decisions about money are weighed down with feelings. And the feelings evoked during the recovery process—sometimes ancient ones—require a lot of support to process. This is the two-pronged threshold of recovery: practical financial discipline, coupled with acceptance and faith in a new way. Neither one works without the other.

Cultivating a new voice

The voice deep inside each of us runs things in whatever way is necessary to avoid uncomfortable feelings. To take control of our lives, we cultivate a new voice that simply doesn't go by those rules.

The new voice lets that old voice know that we can handle things now. We superimpose new judgment even when we feel the old feelings. The entire recovery plan establishes a big enough sense of self to contain all those overwhelming feelings, so we don't have to act them out.

What level of help, and what type of help will work for each person is essentially an individual question. Every seeker will eventually find the method of support that works best for them. Or perhaps the combination of methods that works best. Of the people I have worked with, there have been as many roads as there have been quests. Many get strength from their chosen religion, or from a new religious or spiritual practice. Prayer and meditation often help. Some open new dimensions in themselves by delving into spirituality or philosophy. Others find a truly wonderful system of support that has often been hidden in plain sight: a simple and honest exchange of feelings with trusted friends and loved ones. Many people seek the help of psychotherapy in conjunction with the practical clarity work. Others go to Debtors Anonymous meetings to join a fellowship of like-minded sufferers. In any case, the two primary fronts that need attention along with the financial work are emotional and spiritual.

Before we start the nuts and bolts of the financial recovery, it has to be clear that it's not about the money. That being said, let's talk about the money. Early attempts to stabilize your finances are usually met with protests from deep inside. You hear something like "I want things my way. I don't like change, and I certainly don't want you unearthing what I've been protecting. My whole purpose is to prevent you from seeing." Clarity develops a new voice, one that says, "Yeah, I hear you. But let *me* take care of us for a while."

The challenge is to cultivate the new voice that is committed to self-care. All the exercises are designed to achieve clarity instead of self-destructive acting out. They deal with money in practical terms—but they are really about developing this new voice. A voice that imposes new judgment. And a voice that incorporates a vision for the future.

Accurate record keeping is the first step

I suggest to everyone I work with that they work on clarity from the very first day. The primary task is to write down every expenditure, every time any money is spent, to the penny. I suggest getting a small book that fits in a pocket or purse.

In other words, if you go to the phone booth and make a call, write it down—"telephone, 25 cents." Stop for a slice of pizza and a Coke? Write it down—"food—restaurant, $2.50." Always to the penny.

I'm often asked, "Why to the penny? Surely the difference between spending $2.50 and spending $2.52 doesn't mean very much in the end?" And for most purposes I suppose that's true. But for *clarity's* purpose the difference between $2.50 and $2.52 is immense. After all, the addicted mind will look for any way to reassert itself. And once it rationalizes away the need to be exact, all manner of excuses will follow. The message that keeping records to the penny sends to the money disorder hiding below is: "I'm not going to let you get even the tiniest foothold."

Knowing exactly where you are is the first step in getting where you want to go

Anyone suffering from a money disorder needs to get on a cash basis. That means no more borrowing from anyone for any reason. Get rid of the credit cards. Call up the creditors and close the accounts. Clearly this suggestion is more urgent for compulsive shoppers, spenders, and debtors than for a workaholic who has never had any trouble with debt. Nevertheless, I strongly recommend stopping the use of credit to anyone suffering from a money disorder. For compulsive debtors or spenders, it is a prerequisite to beginning their recovery. For everyone else it is a powerful tool in achieving clarity, and a proactive way to head off switching from one money disorder to another. Living on a cash basis means only spending by means of cash or check. Every time you write a check or make a deposit into the checking account, you record it in the checkbook (and a running balance is updated); every time you spend cash it is recorded in the little cash book.

By employing this system, there is never any question as to how much money came in or where it came from, nor is there any question about how much money went out or what it was spent on. It's all right there in black and white. Clarity. Leaving the house with a hundred dollars and coming back with no idea where it went is no longer possible. Before keeping accurate records, most people had no real idea of whether they could afford something. Asked, "Can you afford that suit or that vacation or that television," they think, "Do I have the cash or the credit available to buy it?" The notion of considering whether the purchase fits into a total financial picture is foreign.

The next step I suggest to everyone I work with is to *develop a Spending Plan.*

Clarity is the basic building block that allows us to create a Spending Plan. And Spending Plans are the beginning of establishing a supportable financial structure.

Most people have at least some experience with trying to get themselves on a budget. The results are never very encouraging. Budgets don't work. They always feel as if they have been prepared by a chastising parent. A budget says, "You better conserve, there's not enough to go around."

A Spending Plan says something a little different: "I have all this money and I get to choose exactly how to spend it." I know this may sound a bit like semantics. But rest assured, the difference between a budget and a Spending Plan is not semantics. The difference may seem small, but it is immeasurable. Spending Plans have the distinct tincture of our own values and dreams.

The next chapter is devoted to a detailed discussion about how to develop your Spending Plan. For now, though, think of a Spending

Plan as a comprehensive way to take care of yourself without having to borrow money. Here's how it's done: I like to imagine a pile of dollar bills on a table in front of you equaling your monthly income—and you get to choose exactly how to spend them. It may not seem that way sometimes, because it seems as if everyone is making demands and deciding things for you. But they don't decide how to spend your money; you do. I then imagine standing in front of a store that has everything in the world inside—rent, utilities, food, insurance, etc. But there's also Tahitian vacations, DVD players, and new living room furniture: everything. What you want to do is to decide in advance how much from that pile of dollar bills to spend in each department. That is what a Spending Plan does. In making these decisions, we start from scratch. We don't take a current list of debts or expenses and modify from there. A Spending Plan needs to be designed from the ground up.

A spending plan is the primary tool for establishing self-care

I have one basic suggestion: let your heart tell you what has to be taken care of. Let your own well-being be your guide from the very start. Ultimately, although sometimes it is an extreme challenge at the beginning, the Spending Plan should reflect your values, dreams, and desires. It is a tool for integrating your creativity, your unique gifts and skills. Questions something like these can be your guide: What did your childhood dreams of your life look like? (Does your life look anything like that?) What do you dream of achieving or experiencing now? (Are you working toward those things?) What things nourish your soul? (Do you provide them for yourself?) What things express your creativity and individuality? (Do you express them?)

None of this is meant to suggest shirking responsibilities to your creditors. No way. In fact, the only way for the plan to work is to maintain an absolute commitment to repaying your creditors 100 percent of the money due them. (It works—just trust me on this.)

It is only when we take care of our *own* needs that we are truly able to discharge our responsibilities to others. Besides, if you don't take care of yourself, you *fuel* the addictive money cycle rather than break it. It is as if a pressure cooker is put on the back burner and set on low flame. For however long we don't take care of our needs, that is how long the pressure builds up, until the lid blows off. That's when the shopping spree happens, or the credit card vacation can't be resisted, or the feeling that everything is just too overwhelming takes root and then the old voice says, "Why even try?"

The first priority in a spending plan, is taking care of you

Taking care of you means establishing savings you can depend on so you don't ever have to feel as if you're walking along the edge of the abyss. And it means caring for the longings of your heart, and the yearnings of your soul. Clearly, the things that nourish my soul are not going to be the things that nourish yours. Everyone's heart wants to sing a different song. It doesn't matter what the song is; it matters only that you sing it. For instance, if I look around my apartment and I don't see any fresh flowers, and I look to find my theater ticket envelope empty—something is up. Because I love the theater, and because I know that flowers lift my spirits and engage my sense of beauty—something is out of balance when I am not tending those needs.

The rest of the Spending Plan determines how much to spend in all the other categories, acknowledging the fact that you have certain fixed expenses and certain responsibilities, including debt repayment. But we don't forget the axiom that *to break whatever money cycle you're in, the first thing is taking care of your needs first.*

The Spending Plan

OK. Get out a pad and a pen. We're going to do your Spending Plan. Don't worry if you have trouble staying focused, or can't do very much in one sitting—most people find themselves feeling something like that. Give yourself a break, take some deep breaths, go for a walk, come back to it tomorrow. But stick with it. And don't worry if you find yourself feeling confused or flustered about the numbers and the money. Believe me, it's natural. Do your best, and take it at your own pace. At the end you will have something invaluable: a supportable emotional and financial structure.

The first entry at the top of the page will be your income. So write "Net Monthly Income" as your top line, like this:

Net Monthly Income   _____

Fill in the amount you receive after taxes have been deducted. If you are a salaried employee, you would multiply the amount of your net check times how often you are paid. For example, if you are paid weekly, or fifty-two times a year, you would multiply by 4.3 to come up with a monthly income figure. (You use 4.3 instead of 4 because there are fifty-two weeks you get paid each year, not forty-eight.) Therefore, if you are paid every two weeks you would multiply your check by 2.15 to come up with your monthly income. If you are paid once a month or twice a month, you would simply multiply by one or by two. If you own a business, or are self-employed, you would use the average of your net income from the last six months if you can reliably predict it is sustainable over the next six. If not, use your most modest prediction for the next six months. Of course, whenever you are responsible for withholding your own taxes, the most important first step is to make sure the tax deposits are made. You can establish a "tax cave" to keep quarterly taxes in, somewhere you segregate the taxes that will be due. You don't touch it until you pay the taxes.

Your net monthly income is exactly how big the pile of money is that you get to spend in the whole-wide-world store. The rest of the Spending Plan will be your attempt to take care of yourself by carefully spending in each department so that you take care of all your needs (and a lot of your wants), discharge all your responsibilities, and honor the debts to your creditors, without running out of money by the time we get to the checkout counter.

Since we discussed savings as a crucial need in a Spending Plan, we put that next. The Spending Plan now looks like this:

Income
    Net Monthly Income   _____
Expenses
    Savings   _____

As a rule of thumb, I like to save at least one month's expenses each year. That means putting 8 percent of net monthly income into savings. If you are struggling with debt or are in an underearning pattern start with 5 percent, or in a real pinch, make it 2 percent. You can raise it as your income grows. So simply multiply net monthly income by .08 or .05 or .02, as the case may be. If you are contributing to a savings or retirement plan at work, you should not contribute so much that you can't save at least 5 percent in a savings account outside of the plan at work. If you find yourself in that position, just ask the plan administrator to lower your contribution and begin saving the balance in a separate savings account.

The next most important items in a Spending Plan are the things that best take care of you. That make your heart sing. That make you feel good about yourself, or allow you to feel connected to a larger world. That use your skills and talents; that express your creative soul. So, now it looks like this:

Income
   Net Monthly Income   _____
Expenses
   Savings   _____
Taking care of yourself
   Self-care category #1   _____
   Self-care category #2   _____
   Self-care category #3   _____
   Self-care category #4   _____
   Self-care category #5   _____
   Self-care category #6   _____
   Etc.

The overall goal of the Spending Plan is to take care of you. The temptation can be really strong to skimp on this. Don't do it, don't skimp here. If you do, you set the stage for the pressure to build up again, and maybe for the cooker to explode when you least expect it. After all, the instrument with which all responsibilities will be discharged, all debts retired, and through whom all interactions in this world will take place—is you. Taking care of that instrument is job #1.

The next items on the list are your fixed expenses. These are the things that everyone has, more or less. You may not have all of them, and you may have some that are not listed here. Feel free to insert any expenses you have that are not listed, and delete anything you do not have.

Fixed Expenses

    Rent/Mortgage   _____

    Maintenance   _____

    Utilities   _____

    Phone   _____

    Cable   _____

    Internet   _____

    Home Insurance   _____

    Health Insurance   _____

    Disability Insurance   _____

    Car Payment   _____

    Car Expenses (Gas, etc.)   _____

    Car Insurance   _____

    Etc.

To round out the Spending Plan, we add in all the personal items that make up everyday life:

Variable Expenses

    Groceries   _____

    Food—Restaurants   _____

    Household Supplies   _____

    Drugstore—Toiletries   _____

    Clothes   _____

    Entertainment   _____

    Medical, Doctors, Co-pay, etc.   _____

    Dentist   _____

    Prescription Medicine   _____

Therapy _____

Transportation _____

School, Tuition _____

School, Fees, and Costs _____

Exercise, Gym, Fitness _____

Hobbies _____

Professional Fees—Legal, Accounting, etc. _____

Hair, Nails, etc. _____

Grooming, Pampering—Facials, Massage, etc. _____

Dating _____

Gambling _____

Bars, Drinks, etc. _____

Vacations _____

Furniture, Home Improvements _____

Art _____

Gifts _____

Kids—Allowances, Clothes, etc. _____

Parents—or Aid to Other Relatives _____

Etc.

Finding the right amount

The way to figure out the right amount for each category is to figure out how to best take care of yourself and have all your needs met, balanced against how much income there is. You need to ask yourself, "How would I spend in this category if I was taking care of myself—but not indulging myself? How much would it be if I was taking care of myself—but not depriving myself?" This is the rigorous test and retest to submit all categories to: not to skimp, neither to go overboard. It takes honesty, and it takes courage.

I worked with a man who loved the ballet, and that was the first self-care category on his plan. I asked him how much would be the right amount to spend, given his income—an amount that would neither deprive nor indulge him, but would take care of him. He said it wouldn't mean much to him to have anything short of season subscriptions to at least two full repertory companies—and really good seats. I said that would be nice. But when we figured it out, fitting that amount of ballet into his plan seemed fairly difficult, given that it would probably cost $3,600—about 12 percent of his net income—to buy that number and quality of seats. "Ok, forget the ballet then," he said.

But that's not the way to go at all. We needed to make sure he got to go to his treasured ballet, not "all or nothing" as was his impulse. We worked out a plan for him to go to a performance every six weeks or so—at about $40 per month. He had other grandiose notions of what would take care of him that led him to take the same "all or nothing" attitude in several self-care categories; using the same strategy, we provided for all of them in the clear light of day.

Be on the lookout for "shoulds"

They can be dangerous places where the Spending Plan gets hijacked by feelings of guilt or shame. "Shouldn't I give my daughter the music lessons she loves?" I was recently asked by a single mother struggling with debt. "Should I deny her the sneakers all her friends wear?" No one wants to deny their children, especially in the areas where they felt denied growing up. The basic reality, however, is that the Spending Plan is not unlimited. Certainly, giving to your children is important, it can be a blessing. It can also feel like a never-ending drain that leaves you in untenable financial straits. I told her that of course it was reasonable to give to her daughter, but I also told her I thought it was unreasonable to give so much that it caused her overall Spending Plan to jump the tracks.

No expense is literally "fixed"

I worked with a man who had an apartment that he clearly could not afford and continue to have anything like an abundant life. Actually, he couldn't afford it without continually going into debt.

Nonetheless, he insisted that the mortgage on the apartment was a "fixed" expense and could not be changed. Despite knowing the devastating results his continued debting was visiting on the rest of his life, he could not bring himself to confront the feelings that kept him married to the apartment. Until he accepted that truth and was willing to move from the apartment that was the albatross around his neck, he stayed in his addictive money cycle. I'm not suggesting you need to move to break whatever cycle you are in. But certainly he had to. I simply want to point out that whenever there is a category that feels as if you could "never" change it—pay attention. There is probably some kind of heat there. Some categories take extraordinary courage to change: often they are the very categories that when changed, open up great stores of energy. But no category is literally "fixed."

So the Spending Plan looks like this:

Income
 Net Monthly Income   _____
 Other Income—Investments, Savings, etc.   _____
 Total Income   _____
Expenses
 Savings   _____
Taking care of yourself
 Self-care category #1   _____
 Self-care category #2   _____
 Self-care category #3   _____
 Self-care category #4   _____
 Self-care category #5   _____
 Self-care category #6   _____
Fixed Expenses
 Rent/Mortgage   _____
 Maintenance   _____
 Utilities   _____

Phone   _____

Cable   _____

Internet   _____

Home Insurance   _____

Health Insurance   _____

Disability Insurance   _____

Car Payment   _____

Car Expenses—(Gas, etc.)   _____

Car Insurance   _____

Etc.

Variable Expenses

Groceries   _____

Food—Restaurants   _____

Household Supplies   _____

Drugstore—Toiletries   _____

Clothes   _____

Entertainment   _____

Medical, Doctors, Co-pay, etc.   _____

Dentist   _____

Prescription Medicine   _____

Therapy   _____

Transportation   _____

School, Tuition   _____

School, Fees, and Costs   _____

Exercise, Gym, Fitness   _____

Hobbies   _____

Professional Fees—Legal, Accounting, etc.   _____

Hair, Nails, etc.   _____

Grooming, Pampering—Facials, Massage, etc.   _____

Dating   _____

Gambling   _____

Bars, Drinks, etc.   _____

Vacations   _____

Furniture, Home Improvements	_____
Art	_____
Gifts	_____
Etc.	
Total Expenses	_____
Total Income	_____
Balance (Total Income minus Total Expenses)	
available to pay creditors	_____
Or, if no creditors	
the same balance to invest, etc.	_____

That is the basics of how to establish a Spending Plan. Most people don't find their first attempt works very well. If you are an overspender, you are fairly likely to have your expenses add up to more than your income. If you are an anorectic spender, you're more likely not to spend anywhere near enough to take care of yourself. After you go all the way through for the first time, you have the chance to refine the plan and make sure it does everything you need it to.

Adjusting the spending plan: when you need to cut back

If the expenses you set down are more than your income, go back to the beginning and rework some categories to bring them into alignment. Don't simply get rid of categories. That is the natural inclination—to simply slash and burn certain things. Inevitably, your first inclination will be to get rid of self-care categories. Or to give disproportionate weight to the categories that have become the most habitual in your life. I remember a woman who was way over in expenses the first time through, and going back was looking everywhere to get rid of things in order to preserve what she saw as indispensable, her "hair" category, at an admittedly rather high $625 per month. That's not the way to do it. If $625 is the right amount to take care of you at the hairdresser—fine. So be it. But not if that would mean lots of other categories would need to be artificially low, or if it means sacrificing other self-care areas.

Try to reduce several categories. For instance, if your expenses are $150 more than your income—you might consider reducing 10 categories by $15 each, rather than looking to get rid of a $150 category. That way, you are more likely to find that elusive quality— balance.

I recently worked with a woman who could not see her way clear to bring her classical CD buying category down below $500 per month. I asked her which composers she bought. I asked how often she went to the music store. I asked her how much she would spend in her CD category if she were taking care of herself but not indulging herself. She said $500 per month was the absolute minimum. I told her I thought we were mining a rich vein, since I am always on the lookout for categories that feel sacrosanct—ones that can't be touched. I asked her what it would feel like if she didn't buy *any CDs* for the next ninety days. She began to cry. I asked her what she was feeling. "I feel like I would be set adrift in a sea where there is no finding the shore. I feel like I would be all alone, disconnected, and afraid. Like I would lose my only friend."

Pay dirt. She had just elucidated more beautifully than I ever could the dilemma of the compulsive debtor. She wants $500 worth of CDs per month, she can't afford $500 worth of CDs per month—and she can't tolerate that feeling. Once we had discussed the source of her need to keep this category so high—her feelings of being alone in the world, without friends and a feeling of connection—she was able to see that it was probably not *through CDs* that she could best find these things. Right then, some of the heat came off her demands to keep her music buying at such a high level. All of a sudden, buying one or two CDs a week felt just right to her. So her classical music category went from $500 to $100 in that instant. Not every category resolves so easily, but they can all be reworked to take care of your needs, reasonably.

In another, slightly lighter example, a man I worked with had a category for "Double Mocha Cappuccinos." He liked to take coffee breaks three times a day, and at each one he bought himself his favorite Double Mocha Cappuccino—at $5.50 a pop. He thought, "I deserve to have whatever coffee I like. I work like a dog. After all, I earn almost fifty thousand dollars a year—surely I can afford to buy myself coffee." The problem is that his "Double Mocha Cappuccino" category went like this: three Double Mochas a day times approximately twenty-two working days a month equals $341. Feelings about his Double Mochas aside for the moment; his salary was $49,000, which, since he lived in New York City, netted him $36,000 after taxes. Take home pay—$3,000 per month, Double Mocha Cappuccino category— $341 per month. His Double Mocha category came down to approximately 10 percent of his take-home pay. Maybe that's all right in the scheme of things, but probably not.

The primary task is to make sure that before we get to the checkout counter in the everything-in-the-world store, that we take care of our needs and our responsibilities. And not borrow to do so. Remember, we don't borrow anymore no matter what. And a big part of our responsibility is our Debt Repayment Plan (a full discussion a bit later).

Adjusting the spending plan: when you need to spend more

It is important to remember that it is not only decreasing certain categories, but increasing others, that makes for a successful Spending Plan. I worked with a young workaholic lawyer who was juggling a million balls in the air and surely needed to review some of the outrageous expenses that were keeping him in debt. But when I questioned him about things that touched him or moved him, he became silently wistful and eventually invited me into the reverie. "I was thinking about the sculpting I loved doing so much when I was in college, and about how much I missed it." "Make a sculpture category immediately," I told him. "How can I find the time?" he lamented. "Find the time," I said.

Time is a crucial component of a Spending Plan and apportioning it wisely can be as important as apportioning the money. Time problems are only a slightly more subtle way of depriving one's self. The feeling that there is never enough money is pretty much the same as the feeling that there is never enough time. And the two can form a powerful alliance. This is especially true when there doesn't seem to be enough time for the things that take care of you. It is also an especially salient feature in underearning, when time that should be charged for isn't, or when your time is undervalued.

Austerity spending plans

Once a review of the finances is complete, sometimes an Austerity Spending Plan is called for. This is a Spending Plan designed to get you over a rough patch but still committed to taking care of you. If your income is not up to where a reasonable Spending Plan can be accomplished, you devise a Spending Plan that is temporary, until you are on your feet. In this case we still don't get rid of the things that take care of you, because to do so would reinforce the vicious cycle rather than break it. What we do is cut everything back to what is absolutely necessary to take care of you, while not incurring any debt to do so. Maybe clothes can wait a while. Maybe books can be read at the library. Maybe even rent can be put off in extreme cases, if other lodgings can be arranged. In any case, the operative idea here is to be creative. And to be patient. This stuff does work.

"What if after taking care of myself and my responsibilities, I have a negative balance?" "What if paying the bills leaves me nothing to pay my debts?" These are two very frequently asked questions. Indeed, if we are dealing with compulsive spending, shopping, or debting, it is very frequently the case that not only is there no balance left at the end of the Spending Plan, it is more likely there is a shortfall, sometimes a huge shortfall. The same thing is true for compulsive underearners. They may be squeaking by on what they earn, maybe without borrowing, but they rarely are taking good care of themselves. So what about the debt? I will devote the next chapter to the issue of debt, fashioning debt repayment plans, and how to work with your creditors the Spending Plan way.

Dealing with Creditors

If debt is a problem, I suggest the discussion in this chapter to everyone as a guide to retiring their debt and dealing with their creditors.

Once a Spending Plan is established that takes care of your needs, then it's time to look at your list of creditors and to come up with a plan for repaying them. Note that until now there was no place on the Spending Plan for debt repayment. That was on purpose. The way to retire your debt while working a Spending Plan is to develop the Spending Plan to take care of your needs first and, only then, to repay all creditors on a pro-rata basis with the available balance left after the Spending Plan is in place.

So, make a list of your creditors, how much you owe to each, how much is available to repay creditors in total, and how much is each creditor's pro-rated amount apportioned to them each month. Here is an example:

Creditor	Amount Owed	Percentage of Total Debt	Payment
Visa	$2,000	10%	$50
MasterCard	$11,000	55%	$275
Amex	$1,000	5%	$25
Macy's	$2,000	10%	$50
Discover	$3,000	15%	$75
Parents	$1,000	5%	$25
Total Debt	$20,000	100%	Total available $500 to pay all debt

This is what a repayment plan to each creditor would look like if the total debt owed to all creditors is $20,000, and the total amount available to repay creditors at the end of the Spending Plans is $500.

"What if those repayment amounts are nowhere near what creditors are demanding as minimum payments?"

It is important to be open and honest with all your creditors. An integral part of paying creditors back according to a repayment plan is staying in touch with them, apprising them of your situation, and being responsive to their calls and letters. In other words, if you are proposing to pay less than the minimum payments to your creditors according to the dictates of your Spending Plan, you must open up an honest communication with them.

First, call or write to each creditor and tell them of your situation and of your commitment to repaying them the full amount you owe. Confirm the amount. Then, tell them that you've found yourself in a problem cycle with money you are attempting to break, and that you

have only a certain amount to pay them if you are going to success-
fully stop the cycle. Stick to your amount.

Tell them that you are sending them the first check and that you
will faithfully send checks every month until the debt is repaid. You
are not seeking to get them to agree with the amount you propose—
they probably won't. You are simply telling them what you are able to
do now, if you are going to avoid going right back into the addictive
cycle. Tell them that if your circumstances change, and you are able to
repay at a higher rate, that they will be the first to know. Tell them
that they should feel free to write or call you, and you will answer
them promptly. But stick to your repayment plan as dictated by your
Spending Plan. (A note about repaying more if circumstances
improve: only do so if the amount available to repay all creditors gets
substantially higher and stays so for at least a period of six months.
Then be sure it seems reasonable to predict that the new levels feel
reasonably stable.) At that point you will have done everything in
your power to do, the rest is not up to you—you cannot, and need not,
control their response. You just need to keep taking the best actions
you know how, regardless of their response.

There is never any reason for you to tolerate abusive behavior from
collection agents or attorneys. No way. But it is wise to remember
that debtors generally feel as if all their creditors are abusive. There
are rules that collection people have to follow, by law. They can't
bother you at work, they can't tell your friends or co-workers about
your debt, they can't call before eight in the morning or after ten at
night, they can't call more than twice in a given week, and they certainly can't threaten or harass you. If they do any of those things, tell
them to stop. If they continue, tell them they are breaking the law and
to stop contacting you.

However, if they are being persistent and reasonable, and not abusive—but that makes you feel afraid or ashamed, and you aren't able
yet to bear that pressure very well—keep a card to read to them under

the phone, so that you can use it to end a conversation that has become overwhelming. After all, you owe them some money—you don't owe them your life. Therefore, if the conversation gets heated, and the collection person doesn't seem to want to accept what you are telling them, read from a card that says something like: "I hear what you are saying. I remain committed to paying back the debt I owe you in full. I am only able to pay $_____ at the moment. I will stay in touch with you. Thank you. Good-bye." And *politely* hang up. There is no reason to keep talking if no one is listening.

Set up a file for each creditor, and keep a record of each contact you have with each one. Keep copies of all correspondence from both sides. Transcribe each conversation, with the date and name of contact, on a separate sheet of paper. And, of course, keep a list of all payments made, and the new amount owed. This is the way to keep clarity about your creditors, your debts, their retirement, and your willingness to keep up an open and honest interchange. Keeping all records extremely clear is an essential part of clarity with creditors.

"What if I have no money left to pay creditors after establishing my Spending Plan?"

It is by no means uncommon for a compulsive debtor, or for a compulsive underearner, to have, at least temporarily, no money at all available to pay creditors. That does not mean that the Spending Plan has been ill-conceived or that it is unworkable, neither does it mean that you should go back and reduce categories even more so that you can start repaying debt. No. Obviously we're talking about being reasonable. You can't have a Porsche in the driveway and tell your creditors you don't have any money available to pay them. If, after being as searching and as reasonable as you can in establishing your Spending Plan to meet your needs and your reality, you still have no money available for a repayment plan to your creditors—then you can't pay them anything yet. Do call them, however. Request a ninety-day moratorium on repaying your debt. Request it in writing, certified mail, return receipt requested. Get back in touch with them in ninety days and tell them whether you can start repayments yet. When you are able to begin, follow the blueprint above for repaying.

"What if one or more of my debts are taxes I owe to the government?"

This is an area that needs careful consideration. It would be great if all creditors were created equal, but they are not. Unfortunately, it doesn't work that way. Taxing authorities, including the IRS and city and state revenue departments, are in a different category, by virtue of the fact that they do not have to go through a long legal process to collect what is owed them. Furthermore, if they disagree with the amount you propose to pay based on your Spending Plan, they can simply say no, and then go about attaching bank accounts, salaries, etc.

But wait. All that is theoretically true, but in practice it is not so scary. The IRS and other tax agencies tend to respond well to people coming to them honestly. I'm not guaranteeing how any given agent will respond on any given day, but my experience after working with many, many people in debt with their taxes is that taxing authorities can be, and generally are, as reasonable as any other creditor. Sometimes more so.

The key, I have found, is to humbly ask them for help. It is imperative to establish how much your repayment plan to the IRS or any local taxing authority will be before establishing a repayment plan with your other creditors. The simple reason is that eventually the other creditors can only be paid on a pro-rated basis after you know how much is still available after the tax repayments are settled. I recommend calling or preferably going to the IRS or state or city and asking to see an agent. Tell him the same thing you would tell any creditor: that you have run into some difficulties and are attempting to straighten them out. Ask them for their help, obviously in your own words, but by saying something like this: "I need your help. I owe $_____ in taxes and I have found myself in a money cycle that I am attempting to break.

I would like to begin a repayment plan, but I can only afford $_____ (tell them the amount your Spending Plan allows on a pro-rated basis). Can you help me, tell me what I should do?"

See what they say. It is likely that they will have you fill out a form requesting an installment payment plan. You will have done most of the work in your Spending Plan. If you run into a hard-nosed agent, tell him you would like to have another agent assigned to your case. It is entirely likely you will get a different agent next time anyway. If you like the agent and he seems particularly helpful—ask how you can stay in touch directly in the future.

I worked with a woman not long ago who was told after a meeting with the IRS to which she brought her accountant and her attorney, that the minimum per month they would accept was $2,800. She could not afford anything like that. After I told her I thought the original meeting might have set her up as an adversary to the IRS, she went back alone and with some humility, and made a personal plea to the agent to help her out of what was a tight spot. The response she got could not have been more different. She told him the amount she had available according to her Spending Plan, and he said, "Are you sure you can actually afford that much?" The repayment she proposed, and he responded to, was $175 per month.

Once you have established repayment plans for whatever taxes are owed, you then know how much is truly available for all other debts. Only then can you set up repayment plans with your other creditors.

"What about my credit rating?"

Many people are worried about what will happen to their credit rating if they don't accede to the demands of their creditors. The notion of protecting their credit rating keeps a lot of compulsive debtors imprisoned in their addictive cycles. "How will I be able to buy a house if I ruin my credit?" "I was always taught that your credit rating is one of the most important things for a person to protect." First, if you are in trouble with debt, your credit rating is already *de facto* ruined. You just don't know it yet. Maybe the chickens haven't all come home to roost just yet, but they're on their way, and they'll be there soon enough. It is just a question of how much maneuvering and finagling, and more debt building, you want to do before you break the cycle. If you already can't afford to pay your creditors, borrowing more will not be the answer. The situation only gets worse, never better. Not taking care of your needs in order to pay your creditors would be an even worse answer in the long run. Will your credit rating suffer? Sure. But a bad rating won't be fatal. I have worked with scores of people who have gotten their financial lives back in order and who subsequently were able to buy houses, etc. Besides, if you are committed to living on a cash basis and not borrowing anymore— except for buying a house or a car—exactly what do you need your credit rating for anyway?

Some people are deeply concerned about interest on their outstanding debt continuing to pile up. Some repayment plans, by necessity, are small enough that the interest is higher each month than the payment, and the debt balance just keeps getting higher. That can lead to feelings of being overwhelmed, even hopeless. It is my experience that those feelings are just that—feelings.

I have watched many people who felt absolutely imprisoned by their debt subsequently feel no pressure whatsoever after diligently using this recovery process. I have watched people who could not realistically expect to pay back their debt in this lifetime live a productive, abundant life—and even they do not necessarily feel pressure from or threatened by debt anymore. The key is not how fast you get rid of the debt. The key is how well you live life. Living according to a Spending Plan that takes care of your needs, and repaying your creditors is the only way reasonably possible to avoid reigniting the addictive cycle.

After making regular payments, usually for a period of one or two years—some people are able to get their creditors to reduce, or forgive entirely, the interest on the debt. I remember a middle-aged single mother who was worried about being able to afford college for her daughter. She made a call to every one of her creditors to tell them about her new, supportable financial structure, and her commitment not to incur any new debt, as well as to retiring all her old debt. She asked each of them for their help. She described her situation. You might be surprised at her results. Not every creditor reduced her interest—but most did. And even the ones who didn't complimented her on her regular and prompt payments. This made her feel that a very large change had taken place in her position in the world and her relating to other people without fear.

"Lawsuits scare me to the bone. Just the threat of them scares me. What do I do about aggressive creditors who threaten to sue?"

This is another area that keeps compulsive debtors locked in their addictive cycles—fear of lawyers, lawsuits, judges, and judgments. Here's the deal: you are only responsible for your side of the street in these transactions. It is your responsibility to be open and honest about your position. It is your responsibility to establish a reasonable Spending Plan that takes care of your needs but doesn't shirk your responsibilities. It is your responsibility to remain committed to repaying your debt 100 percent; after all, you incurred it. Again, it is most definitely not, however, your responsibility, nor is it in your power, to control the way any given creditor responds.

Each creditor acts differently, but most have certain things in common. They tend to resist accepting smaller payments at first—they send stern letters, threaten to refer you to the legal department, and use whatever means they have at hand to get you to come up with the money. Some increase the pressure, others make offers to accept a payoff of between 40 and 70 percent of the entire debt, if you will pay it all immediately. Sometimes these offers are powerfully enticing—getting out from under a chunk of debt at a 30 to 60 percent discount? Wow. But where would the money come from? If you were able to pay back all your debt without borrowing, or without some other draconian measure, you would have done it by now. Some people are tempted to transfer that amount to a new credit card, especially one with a lower interest or introductory rate. Don't do it. My experience is that borrowing from anyone at all after you have begun the process, even if it seems logical, is a very dangerous and slippery slope. It allows that addictive inner voice to get a foothold again. And, before you even know it, you're off to the races again.

Ultimately, creditors understand that they will have to accept smaller payments from some people until they are back on their feet. Most creditors accept this fact.

It is wise to remember, however, that collection agents typically earn their living on commission—the more they collect, the more they earn. Hence the aggressive stance some of them take. They are also well trained in the art of coercing debtors into paying even when they can't afford to, by evoking guilt and shame.

I remember a particular creditor of mine who was calling when I was fielding calls from all my creditors, and they were giving me a more or less full-time stomachache. I called it my debt stomachache. This particular guy seemed to sense how vulnerable I was, and he was able to get straight through to my gut, to easily evoke how terrible I felt about myself. He left one particular message on my answering machine that I'll never forget: "I see you still have an answering machine. Don't you?" The message, seemingly, was that if I was a man, I would sell it and everything else—in order to pay him. But wait. There isn't much practical reality there, just shame and guilt. I don't guess there is a very active secondary market in used answering machines. And even if there were, I wonder what exactly his fair pro-rated share of the maybe five bucks it would bring would be? Nevertheless, some part of me identified completely with his disdain for my not paying, and I felt absolutely terrible about myself despite how ludicrous his suggestion was in the real world.

If you do your part diligently, most creditors will not sue. And even if they do—and even if they win—most judges, in my experience, will not upset an overall plan to repay everyone equitably, just to favor the one creditor who would not accept the deal and went to court. So, even given a creditor with a judgment in hand, it is fairly likely that you would wind up after the whole long process having to pay exactly the same amount you proposed in the first place! It doesn't always work out that way—but it sure works out that way pretty darned often. I put it to you—and I have seen judges, annoyed, put it to the creditor this way—what else is realistically possible? Are they suggesting you pay them more, proportionally, than other creditors? Are they suggesting you live like a pauper until their debt is paid off, thereby encouraging the cycle to resume all over again? I think not.

Additionally, there is no real need to hire a lawyer to defend you in a lawsuit of this kind. Feel free to hire one, but in my experience, if you are honestly and humbly presenting yourself to the creditor, and to the court, it oftentimes works out better to represent yourself. Especially since you are not contesting the facts of the case—you admit you owe the money. The only disagreement is over your contention that you can't pay them back as fast as they would like you to.

"Is it ever all right to give a particular creditor favorable treatment and pay them faster than the others?"

The answer is yes. But I hesitate to simply say yes, because the answer is yes only under certain circumstances, and debtors love to contrive circumstances that suit exactly what they wanted to do anyway, instead of following the plan for recovery. I have often come across circumstances in which it becomes perfectly reasonable to pay one creditor faster than the others. Most of the time that is not the case, but sometimes it is. I think the guideline to use is this: if a judge, reviewing the reason to make an exception in the case of this particular creditor, would tend to agree with you, then do it.

"I've heard so much about debt consolidation. Is that a good idea?"

You can hardly turn on the television, or drive by the billboards these days, without being inundated with offers to consolidate your debt. "In trouble with your debt? Come to us for lower payments." "Use the equity in your home to have all your credit card bills read zero next month. Imagine what a relief that would be."

There is a huge market for debt consolidation, because there are a huge amount of people in trouble with debt. Basically, there are two types of companies offering debt consolidation services. The first are essentially mortgage companies offering to put a second mortgage on your house, if you own one. They market themselves as debt consolidators, because that is the way they get the most customers. If you take them up on their offer, they do in fact loan you enough money to pay off your credit card debts (providing you have a good enough credit rating and income, and there is enough equity in your home), and what you then have is a longer-term loan for the same amount, which means that your payments are lower, and presumably more manageable. That is the goal of debt consolidation—lower payments.

The problem with this deal is that it tends to backfire. If your history is one of compulsively incurring debt over a period of time, it is highly unlikely that taking a debt consolidation loan will stop that compulsion. Even if you were to receive a windfall of money you *did not have to repay*, it would not stop the compulsion. Remember, money disorders are not about money—they are about your relationship to it. Therefore, any solution that doesn't hit hard at the underlying causes does not tend to hold water for very long. A year or two down the road, I see people who have taken second mortgages on their houses in order to consolidate their debts. They come to me truly beaten. Now not only do they have an unmanageable debt load because, of course, their debting started up again, but they are being threatened with foreclosure and eviction from their homes.

Debt consolidation isn't always a bad thing—only for people with money disorders. It is perfect for people who have a single episode that puts them in debt—maybe a family member needed an operation, or a hurricane blew the roof off their house, or whatever. If you are in that category, then a debt consolidation loan may be for you. But if you are in the much bigger category of people whose troubles with debt have been more of an ongoing syndrome, more like a pattern in their lives—then a debt consolidation loan will be just one more debt to deal with. And, inevitably, the pattern of incurring debt begins again.

The other type of companies offering debt consolidation are quasi-governmental, or at least nonprofit agencies set up with different names in each state, along the lines of Consumer Credit Counseling or Budget and Credit Counseling Services. These agencies offer a program for consolidating debt that has nothing to do with home equity or mortgages. They have decided, just like the advertisers of second mortgages have, that the only thing people in trouble with debt really need is lower payments. Toward this end, they have you come to them with all your debts and all your expenses figured out. They sit with you and use computerized formulas to figure out what you can afford to pay your creditors each month, and they have you make one payment for that amount to them—and they then pay all your creditors their share of the lower amount. They actually do all the negotiating with the creditor for you. And they charge a small fee for their services.

The problem with these debt counseling services is that they never get down to what is really wrong. That is why their results are predictably short-lived—because they haven't addressed the addictive cycle at its root causes. This is too bad. I believe that agencies of this type could do some real good if they acknowledged the nature of what is driving their clients to continue debting. It's called addiction. I can't tell you how many times someone has come to me months, or perhaps a year or two, after they went to one of these agencies and had their debt consolidated. Why do they come to see me? Because they are in bigger trouble than ever. Just as with a second mortgage, if you get back into your cycle again and start building up the debt again, you will ultimately have the consolidated payment to make, plus all the new payments. And you will not have gotten down to causes. It bears repeating: breaking an addictive money cycle cannot be done by simply paying down your debt.

"A friend of mine suggested I just go bankrupt since my situation seems so unsolvable. Is that a good way to take care of debt that seems impossible to pay back?"

There are lots of bankruptcies because there are lots of people in trouble with debt. One in every forty-five families has filed for bankruptcy in the last three years alone. One in forty-five! That's an astonishing number. A bankruptcy court judge recently told me that she wished that the people she discharges in bankruptcy court could get treatment for their underlying causes instead for what is really wrong. But all she can do is rule on whether certain debts are dischargeable or not within the law—not on whether the debtor should seek some other form of help. The idea of a fresh start is deeply rooted in our history and culture. But the fresh start after a bankruptcy is very often an illusion.

The notion that an individual might lose all hope and opportunity after unforeseeable financial setbacks is the animating idea behind the fresh start of bankruptcy. But it is not unforeseeable setbacks that bring most people to bankruptcy court; it is addictive problems with money and debt. Bankruptcy is not the solution to a money disorder. I am not opposed to bankruptcy, but it is not a solution to a money disorder.

For the first time in a very long time, the very definition of what constitutes a "fresh start" under the federal bankruptcy regulations has been called into question. At this writing, both the House and the Senate have passed their own differing bills, deciding who will continue to qualify for a so-called Chapter 7 bankruptcy in which most debts are discharged (very few people), and who will be required to file under Chapter 13 of the bankruptcy code, requiring repayment of some or all of most debts (which will apply to most people). Needless to say, the credit card companies are not unhappy about this new arrangement. In fact, they were at the center of the lobbying effort to pass the bill in the first place. (The brightest spot in the new bills, from my viewpoint, is that both the House and Senate versions require some form of counseling.)

"Why should I save while I'm still in debt? Isn't that silly? It feels a little futile before the debt is resolved."

I'll close the discussion of debt and creditors by addressing this very important question. Savings is the first line item under expenses on the Spending Plan. This is deliberate. The commitment to stop incurring any debt, and to repay all your creditors one day at a time, accomplishes the goal of capping your debt where it is. I imagine building a concrete wall around the debt on all sides, completely enclosing it. The thing to say to yourself then is: "I will not add any more debt to that pile—from now on it will only go in one direction: down."

On the day you make the commitment not to incur any more debt, make another commitment: to begin saving. I imagine another pile alongside the pile of debt—this is a pile of savings, and while the debt pile is continually going down, the savings is continually going up. The worst thing I can imagine is to slowly retire your debt and have a total of zero savings the day you accomplish that goal. The very worst part of that scenario is having no savings, no feeling of comfort and security, while the debt is being retired. So begin saving the day you end debting. It is deeply important to couple savings with any plan to repay creditors. Typically, Spending Plans call for saving between 5 and 10 percent of net earnings. But even if you can only realistically put five dollars away—do it. Begin. And stick with it. You are saving money you can depend on in emergencies: money you can use for hopes and dreams and for your heart's desires. The mere act of saving creates a very real psychic shift. The idea that your life should be on hold until you pay off your debt, or at least that you shouldn't *save* money until then, is just another way the inner voice of addiction asserts itself. That inner voice is always lurking around, hoping against hope to find some new way to convince you that your life isn't worth living to its fullest.

Don't believe it.

Working with the Spending Plan

Once you've created your Spending Plan, the goal will be to try to spend your money according to the plan all the way through the month. No one gets this right from the start. In fact, we don't ever get it 100 percent right. Rather like "true north" on a compass, the plan is what we aim for, not what we expect to achieve. Nevertheless, our goal is to get closer and closer each month, until, after a while, working with it begins to be like second nature. Until then, the way to ensure that the process stays on track is to monitor it.

So, let's go back to that little book where you are writing down everything you spend. Unless you check to see whether you are actually spending as you planned, the Spending Plan becomes just another intention that you didn't follow through on. The way to turn an intention into a practical reality is to monitor the results.

To do this, you will need a six-column ledger book (I promise—this is the last book). The ledger book is where you combine your cash book and your checkbook into a review. Every week, you total each category and put the categories on a spreadsheet like the one below.

By tracking the progress, you can see that if you've spent $45 of your $50 restaurant category in the first week, then you can only spend $5 more for the month if you intend to stick with your plan. And for the plan to work, you need to stick with it in all categories. Next month, you'll know to keep an eye on the restaurant category. If, on the other hand, you've only rented two videos in a $50 entertainment category, and it's near the end of the month, you better get to spending some entertainment bucks if you're going to stick with the plan. It turns out that when we spend zero or near zero in a category in which spending on yourself becomes hard, that category deserves special attention. It is the zeros that are more indicative of the deeper trouble than the categories that are over the top.

The spreadsheet looks like this:

Categories	Plan	Week 1	Week 2	Week 3	Week 4	Total
Net Income	$2,500	$1,250		$1,250		$2,500
Savings	$200	$50	$50	$50	$50	$200
Self-Care						
Flowers	$50	$25	$8	$9	$7	$49
Movies	$35	$0	$0	$8	$8	$16
Museums	$20	$0	$0	$0	$10	$10
Photography	$30	$15	$15	$0	$15	$45
Fixed Expenses						
Rent	$916	$916	$0	$0	$0	$916
Electric	$60	$0	$51	$0	$0	$51
Cable	$27	$27	$0	$0	$0	$27
Phone	$50	$44	$0	$0	$0	$44
AOL	$20	$20	$0	$0	$0	$20
Insurance	$65	$0	$65	$0	$0	$65
Everyday						
Groceries	$145	$58	$26	$79	$14	$177
Restaurants	$170	$36	$19	$55	$31	$141

Transportation	$63	$63	$0	$0	$0	$63
Clothes	$75	$0	$0	$99	$32	$131
Movies	$16	$0	$0	$9	$0	$9
Laundry	$12	$7	$0	$0	$7	$14
Flowers	$25	$0	$0	$0	$0	$0
Stationery	$19	$0	$0	$0	$0	$0
Supplies	$25	$37	$0	$0	$0	$37
Haircuts	$35	$0	$35	$0	$0	$35
Drugstore	$40	$22	$0	$23	$0	$45
Vacations	$60	$0	$0	$0	$0	$0
Gym	$31	$31	$0	$0	$0	$31
Gifts	$45	$0	$25	$0	$0	$25
Miscellaneous	$25	$11	$7	$0	$2	$20
Total Expenses	$2,258	$1,359	$301	$332	$176	$2,168
Total Income	$2,500					
Repayment Plan	$242					
Amex 34%	$82	$0	$0	$0	$82	$82
Visa 22%	$53	$0	$0	$0	$53	$53
MCard 17%	$41	$41	$0	$0	$0	$41
Loan 27%	$66	$66	$0	$0	$0	$66
Debt Repaid	$242					$242

Remember that this is an overall plan for taking care of you. It is important that you don't spend the entertainment money on clothes, or the art lesson money on restaurants. You don't simply want to make sure you spend less in the categories you tend to go overboard on; instead, you want to give at least as much attention to making sure you spend enough in the self-care categories where you have been known to deprive yourself.

It is equally important to remember that resistance is natural. Slip-ups and mistakes are just that—nothing unforgivable. If you forget to keep your records for a day, just keep them the next day. The natural tendency is to say, "I screwed up. I knew this would work for other people, but never for me." Don't listen to that voice. That is the voice of the part of you that wants things the old way. Just start again. No matter how badly things get fouled up, you can always start the whole process again clean, right now.

When I met Karen she was feeling pretty bad about herself. She had moved from another town and accepted a lesser-paying job in order to live with her new boyfriend. The relationship wasn't going as well as she had hoped and they fought about money all the time. She was doing a high-wire act in order to make all the minimum payments on her credit cards, and taking care of herself was about the last thing on her mind. All she knew was that she wanted to get out from under the pressure the debt had created.

When we first met, her spending looked something like this:

Salary	$38,000 per year
Net Monthly Income	$2,316
Expenses	
Visa	$136
MasterCard	$152
Discover	$89
Student Loan	$216
Payments on past dental work	$200
Rent	$525
Electric/Gas	$75
Phone	$150
Cable	$36
Internet	$11
Car Payment	$235
Car Expenses—Gas, etc.	$70
Car Insurance	$60
Food	$600
Drinks after work	$175

Household Supplies	$35
Drugstore—Toiletries	$70
Clothes	$200
Movies, Videos	$20
Hair, Nails, etc.	$45
Total Expenses	$3,100
Total Income	$2,316
Amount spent more than earned each month	$784

I met her when she had reached the limit on all her credit lines and had gone well beyond the credit limits. After we talked about money disorders and the need to take care of yourself in order to break the cycle, and after she had done a lot of reflecting on her life and the things she wanted to change, she came up with the following plan:

Net Monthly Income	$2,316
Expenses	
Savings	$116
Self-Care	
Ballet	$36
Crafts	$24
Flowers	$21
Photography	$45
Museums	$16
Hiking Vacation	$28
Fixed Expenses	
Rent	$525
Renter's Insurance	$12
Electric/Gas	$75
Phone	$80
Cable	$27
Internet	$11
Groceries	$240

Restaurants	$180
Drinks after work	$70
Household Supplies	$35
Drugstore—Toiletries	$70
Clothes	$85
Movies, Videos	$40
Hair, Nails, etc.	$60
Medical, Doctors, co-pay	$20
Massage	$85
Subway, Bus	$63
Exercise, Gym	$61
Miscellaneous	$20
Total Expenses	$1,844
Total Income	$2,316
Balance available to pay creditors	$472
Debt Repayment Plan	$472

Paid according to the pro-rated formula as follows:

		Payment	% of total debt
Visa	owe $7000	$75	16%
MasterCard	owe $9,000	$94	20%
Discover	owe $5,000	$52	11%
Student Loan	owe $22,000	$216	49%
Dentist	owe $2,000	$19	4%

Karen was committed to not using credit anymore. She knew that breaking her cycle meant reasonably taking care of all aspects of her life—and only then paying her creditors with what was left. Even if that meant needing to contact the creditor to renegotiate payments that were lower than the minimums. So that's exactly what she did. She called each of them to tell them about the situation she had gotten herself into to say that she was now making changes to establish a supportable financial structure, and to specify the amount she could afford to pay in her initial repayment plan.

Look what else she did: she said, "I don't need to pay half of the expenses on an expensive car just because my boyfriend wants it." So she told him that if he wanted to have the car—fine, but that she wasn't willing to pay for it anymore. She began taking the bus and subway instead. She had a look at her phone bill and realized that she made her calls indiscriminately, so she set out how many long-distance minutes she would allow herself with each person. She canceled some of the expanded cable stations. She began cooking at home more. She limited having drinks after work to six times a month. And she made a plan to buy herself an amount of clothes that felt good to her but didn't put undue pressure on the rest of her Spending Plan.

Let's look at yet something else Karen did. She began to take care of herself in all sorts of ways that she had put aside while she was juggling the debt. She started making regular deposits into a savings account. She went back to things she had loved—ballet and sewing; flowers and photography. She admitted a secret desire she had felt guilty about while she had all that debt—she longed to have massages. So she started having a monthly massage. She planned a hiking vacation in the mountains with her boyfriend, and she set aside $28 a month in an envelope marked "hiking vacation." After a year she took that vacation and paid for her half with the cash from her envelope. "Nothing feels better than a paid-up vacation—it isn't anything like the sinking feeling of coming home to the American Express bill for same," she said.

Karen was earning considerably less than someone with comparable experience and talents normally earned. And she wasn't thrilled with the work she was doing in any case. So she decided to ask for a raise—not something that came naturally to her. It took her three weeks to work up the courage, and several test runs with friends to practice her script. At the same time, she put out feelers to everyone she knew to see if they could think of a position for her that would take advantage of her skills and pay her a competitive salary. She spoke to headhunters and looked through job listings on the Internet. Being an underearner, none of this was easy for her, but it sure was esteem-building. Once she was in her boss's office asking for the raise, she knew she wouldn't be happy with less than a 12 percent raise, and she didn't have to accept anything less because she had already found options open to her. She got her raise. Bolstered by her newfound confidence, she also found a much more exciting job less than a year after the raise. At a salary of $60,000.

Richard was also feeling pretty bad about himself when we met. He was a star salesman earning about $100,000 a year. But that hardly insulated him from money problems the way he had once imagined it would. He was working brutally long hours and pushing himself to exhaustion. Nevertheless, the commission checks never could seem to keep up with the bills. His spending at the time was something like this:

Gross Income	$96,000 per year
Net Monthly Income	$6,150
Expenses	
Visa Gold Card	$425
Visa Citibank	$370
Overdraft checking	$211
Line of credit	$650
Optima	$190
His father	Ignoring
Mortgage	$1,260
Electric/Gas	$170
Cable	$54
AOL	$21
Cable modem	$59
Phone	$175
Cell phone	$75
Cell phone — Car	$101
Home insurance	$35

Life insurance	$79
Lawn maintenance	$66
Car payment	$512
Car insurance	$110
Car maintenance/gas, etc.	$120
Food	$950
Clothes	$1,100
Household supplies	$100
Drugstore/toiletries	$125
Kids—allowances	$80
Kids—clothes, etc.	$175
Movies and videos	$140
Books, CDs, subscriptions	$100
Medical, co-pay	$70
Housecleaning	$260
Cigars	$50
Vacations	$350
Total Expenses	$8,183
Total Income	$6,150
Amount spent more than earned each month	$2,033

Relying on his credit cards wasn't enough to sustain his overspending, so Richard went to his father to get bailed out on several occasions. By the time I saw him, he had had it. He was out of the incredible energy it took to keep all the balls in the air. Here are the changes he made:

Gross Income	$96,000 per year
Net Monthly Income	$6,150
Expenses	
Savings	$300
Self-Care	
Golf	$112

Playing the guitar	$60
Concerts	$24
Skiing	$117
Fitness/exercise	$61
Taking classes	$60
Fixed Expenses	
Mortgage	$1,260
Electric/gas	$170
Cable	$54
AOL	$21
Cable modem	$59
Phone	$150
Cell phone	$101
Home insurance	$35
Life insurance	$79
Lawn maintenance	$66
Car payment	$249
Car insurance	$90
Car maintenance/gas, etc.	$120
Food	$850
Clothes	$250
Household supplies	$100
Drugstore/toiletries	$100
Kids—allowances	$80
Kids—clothes, etc.	$75
Movies and videos	$75
Books, CDs, subscriptions	$75
Medical, co-pay	$70
Housecleaning	$130
Cigars	$25
Vacations	$125
Gifts	$75
Miscellaneous	$50

Total Expenses	$5,243
Total Net Income	$6,150
Balance Available to Pay Debt	$907
Debt Repayment Plan	$907

Paid as follows, according to the pro-rated formula:

		Payment	% of total debt
Visa Gold Card	owe $12,000	$118	13%
Visa Citibank	owe $14,000	$136	15%
Overdraft Checking	owe $9,000	$81	9%
Line of Credit	owe $26,000	$245	27%
Optima	owe $5,000	$55	6%
His Father	owe $28,000	$272	30%

After Richard had made these payments religiously for about eighteen months, his father forgave the balance of the debt owed to him. Richard redid his debt repayment plan given the new information (and genuinely thanked his father for the kind offer, rather than feeling shameful whenever he was bailed out). Here's the rearranged repayment plan after his father's loan was forgiven:

Debt Repayment Plan

Visa Gold Card	$163	18%
Visa Citibank	$190	21%
Overdraft Checking	$127	14%
Line of Credit	$354	39%
Optima	$73	8%

About the same time that his father forgave the debt, Richard wrote to all his other creditors asking for whatever relief they could give him from the interest and penalties on his debt. He told them he had stopped borrowing and had been on his new payment plan for eighteen months, but that the high interest made it hard to reduce the debt very much. He asked them for whatever consideration they could give him. One of them just told him where he could get off. But two of them took away all the late charges and fees, as well as bringing his interest back to their lowest level. The other two did something even more surprising: they stopped charging him any interest whatsoever.

Terri owed a lot in back taxes and was afraid to even look at how much. She owns her own business and is very good at what she does. Starting out nineteen years ago, she built a business from scratch that has over a million dollars in sales. Terri's salary from the business has gone from $20,000 a year to $150,000 a year over that time. But she says that each time her salary went into the next bracket, instead of things getting a little easier financially, they kept getting further and further out of hand. She describes it like this: "It's like what they say about a task expanding to the amount of time you allot to it. That's what happens with the money I spend—it expands to the level of my income. Only it expands even further. I've never quite figured out how to live on my take-home pay. No matter how much that take-home pay happens to be."

When I met Terri, she was in debt to a lot of credit cards—but the biggest amount she owed was to the IRS and to state taxes. And she was scared to death to face the situation; she was not at all sure she had enough courage. Neither was she sure that she could handle the intense feelings of shame or the blow to her ego. Here's what happened:

Terri's approximate spending when I met her:

Income

Salary	$150,000 per year
Net Monthly Income	$8,225

Expenses

American Express Platinum	$295
Visa Platinum	$303
MasterCard Gold	$334
Homeowner's line of credit	$218

Saks Fifth Avenue	$95
Neiman Marcus	$190
IRS	Ignoring
State taxes	Ignoring
Mortgage	$2,220
Utilities	$200
Phone	$275
Cable	$90
Internet	$20
Cell phone	$170
Home insurance	$75
Health insurance	$268
Disability insurance	$180
Car payment	$499
Car expenses—gas, etc.	$120
Car insurance	$130
Variable Expenses	
Groceries	$900
Food—restaurants	$650
Household supplies	$100
Drugstore—toiletries	$150
Clothes	$750
Entertainment	$50
Medical, doctors, co-pay, etc.	$50
Prescription medicine	$50
Therapy	$400
Exercise, gym, fitness	$120
Professional fees—legal, accounting, etc.	$125
Hair, nails, etc.	$190
Grooming, pampering—facials, massage, etc.	$125
Acupuncture, alternative healing, body work	$140
Dating	$50
Drinks, bars, etc.	$200

Vacations	$350
Furniture, home improvements	$275
Total Expenses	$10,357
Total Net Income	$8,225
Total amount spent each month more than earned	$2,132

Terri wanted desperately to resolve the problem with her taxes and her other creditors so it wouldn't be hanging over her head anymore like the sword of Damocles. She also knew she needed to establish a supportable plan before she could reasonably approach her creditors. Here's what she came up with:

Income	
Salary	$150,000 per year
Net Monthly Income	$8,225
Expenses	
Savings	$250
Self-Care	
Classical music	$92
Walks in the park	$0
Candles	$ 45
Soaps and creams	$110
Yoga	$120
Cooking	$100
Theater	$ 70
Fixed Expenses	
Mortgage	$2,220
Utilities	$200
Phone	$160
Cable	$ 55
Internet	$ 20
Cell phone	$ 60
Home insurance	$ 75

Health insurance	$268
Disability insurance	$180
Car payment	$499
Car expenses—gas, etc.	$120
Car insurance	$130
Variable Expenses	
Groceries	$425
Food—restaurants	$375
Household supplies	$ 60
Drugstore—toiletries	$ 80
Clothes	$125
Movies and videos	$ 50
Medical, doctors, co-pay, etc.	$ 30
Prescription medicine	$ 50
Therapy	$400
Professional fees—legal, accounting, etc.	$100
Hair, nails, etc.	$120
Facials, massage	$ 75
Acupuncture, alternative healing, body work	$ 70
Dating	$ 50
Vacations	$125
Housecleaning	$240
Miscellaneous	$ 25
Total Expenses	$7,174
Total Net Income	$8,225
Balance Available to Pay Debt	$1,051
Debt Repayment Plan	$1,051

Because Terri's largest debt was taxes, she followed the debt repayment plan in which you make sure you know how much your payments to the IRS and the state will be before making the pro-rated plan with your other creditors. The reason for this is eminently practical: the IRS and the state are in a different category of creditor; they don't have to go to court to win a judgment and they don't have to accept any payment plan other than one that pleases them. That said, they don't tend to be any more demanding than any other creditor; usually they are somewhat more flexible and willing to help.

So Terri went to the IRS and asked the agent assigned to her case for help. She explained that she had been in a self-defeating cycle with money and was getting help rearranging her finances so she could break the cycle she was in. She showed the agent her spending plan and the amounts she owed the other creditors and said she hoped to pay back all creditors proportionally, but that she would accept whatever the agent told her to do. Terri told her the pro-rated share the IRS would get was $368. Terri left the meeting with the IRS agent with a repayment plan of $300 a month. She did the same thing with the state. The agent there wasn't as understanding, and demanded considerably more than the $74 Terri told him would have been the pro-rated share to them. Her repayment plan to the state was $175 a month.

So, with her repayment plans to the IRS and the state in hand, she made her repayment plan as follows:

Debt Repayment Plan	$1,051
IRS	$300
State Taxes	$175
Total Tax repayments	$475
Balance Available	$576
Homeowner's Line of Credit	$218
Balance Available	$358

Paid on a pro-rated basis to the remaining creditors as follows:

		Payment	% other debt
American Express Platinum	owe $13,000	$100	28%
Visa Platinum	owe $14,100	$111	31%
MasterCard Gold	owe $12,700	$100	28%

Saks Fifth Avenue	owe $ 2,200	$18	5%
Neiman Marcus	owe $ 3,800	$29	8%

It took Terri several months to establish her Spending Plan, then to become clear on all the things she needed to do to get a repayment plan that she could stick with. It was not easy for her. "Was it worth it?" she asked herself. "I've never felt so free before in my life—almost like all the impediments to living were removed and the world opened up for the first time."

It can take a while to feel comfortable with all the new disciplines. It can take even a longer while to readily tolerate the feelings that come along with being your own best advocate. Staying on track with a Spending Plan and with a new way of life gets easier and more natural each month. Not only easier and more natural—but eventually, indispensable.

The Time Plan

Workaholics need a Time Plan as much as they need a Spending Plan. So do many people with money disorders. Just as a Spending Plan says, "I have all this money, and I get to choose exactly how to spend it," a Time Plan says, "I have all this *time*, and I get to choose exactly how to spend it." Each statement feels like a trick of semantics the first time we hear it. As with the Spending Plan, the difference is subtle but immeasurable. When we stand outside the whole-wide-world store contemplating our Spending Plan, we decide in advance how much to spend in each department, ensuring that we take care of our needs first, and making sure to fulfill our responsibilities. The same is true with a Time Plan. At the beginning of each week, we *do* have 168 hours to spend, and we *do* get to choose exactly how to spend them. It just doesn't seem that way sometimes.

The animating idea is the same; in order to break the compulsive cycle your needs must come first. The first order of business is to allot time for the things that mean something to you, and time for the things that feed your heart. That time becomes non-negotiable. For a workaholic, making time negotiable automatically means too much of it will be spent working. The Time Plan needs to be non-negotiable, at least at first. Obviously there are exceptions; if an emergency arises, being flexible is what we do. But wait a minute. How many true emergencies are there? Workaholics tend to think of everything as an emergency. The truth is that when there are no more emergencies brewing, they create them, always reinforcing the cycle. Out of emergencies? Well, there are always lots of excuses queued up. "Everyone who gets ahead has to work hard." "With my boss, you either work the hours or you're out." "What could I do, the client needed it yesterday." Always reinforcing the cycle.

Creating a balanced and reprioritized Time Plan is essentially like taking the workaholic's current Time Plan and turning it upside down.

The workaholic's time plan usually looks something like this:

> Work
> Work
> Work
> Other Responsibilities
> Family
> Yourself

Breaking the cycle means making it more like this:

> Yourself
> Family
> Other Responsibilities
> Work

That is how to begin the healing. It is not only too much time that the workaholic spends on work—workaholics have also been known to work with life-force-draining intensity. Of course, they will assure you it is life-force-*giving* intensity. After all, workaholics never feel better than when they're working. That is the crux of the problem.

Workaholics cannot even *imagine* what they would do with their time if they weren't working. The same amount of time and effort spent reflecting on self-care categories in the Spending Plan needs to be spent reflecting and remembering things that are truly meaningful to you in the Time Plan. Those are the things that should get your prioritized time, not work. It will do well for any workaholic to remember that no one in their final days has ever expressed regret this way: "Gee, I wish I had spent more time at work."

Total Hours in a Week   168

All right—calling all workaholics—get out a pad and a pen. Let's do your Time Plan.

Like the Spending Plan, the first categories that get allotments of time in the Time Plan are the ones that take care of you. We need to consider all aspects of you that need to be cared for, then allot an appropriate time for them. You want to consider emotional, physical, and spiritual well-being before you get to professional and financial well-being.

There are two questions to use as your guide: "How much time would I spend on this if I didn't ever *have* to work anymore and have decided *not* to work anymore?" and "How much time would I devote to this if I was taking care of myself and not depriving myself? Taking care of myself, but not indulging myself?" Forget about how many hours work takes up for now. Obviously, workaholics don't tend to overindulge their time allotments for very much besides work. So we concentrate on taking care of you, not depriving you, in each of the self-care categories.

The emotional well-being categories include spending time with your partner, dating, spending time with friends, taking time just for yourself, time for entertainment, time for therapy, time for reading—you know what they are.

The physical well-being categories include: sleeping, resting, exercise, medical checkups, sex, nutrition, eating in a peaceful and restful way . . .

And the spiritual well-being categories are along the lines of time for contemplating beauty, time for religious practice, time for prayer or meditation, time for reflection . . .

Again, you are the instrument that is asked to do all the work. Taking care of your needs first is the only way to break the workaholic cycle.

So, the Time Plan looks like this so far:

Total Hours in a Week	168
Self-Care	
Emotional	_____
Physical	_____
Spiritual	_____

Once you've allotted all the time you need to take care of your needs, then you can turn to the time needed to spend with your family. Ask yourself the same questions: "How much time would I spend with my kids if I was taking care of them and myself, and not depriving myself?" "How much time do I need to devote to my wife? My parents? My cousins? . . . if I was taking care of them and myself, but not depriving myself?"

Now the Time Plan looks like this:

Total Hours in a Week	168
Self-Care	
Emotional	_____
Physical	_____
Spiritual	_____
Family	_____

Now take a look at the other areas in your life outside of work. How much time would you devote to service if you were taking care of yourself and your needs and values and beliefs, and not depriving yourself? How much time would you devote to organizations you believe in or would like to be a member of, if you were taking care of yourself and not depriving yourself?

Now the Time Plan looks like this:

Total Hours in a Week	168
Self-Care	
Emotional	_____
Physical	_____
Spiritual	_____
Family	_____
Other Values	_____

Then, and only then, you allot the time needed for:

Work	_____

So the Time Plan, when finished, has categories like this:

Total Hours in a Week	168
Self-Care	
Emotional	_____
Physical	_____
Spiritual	_____
Family	_____
Other Values	_____
Work	_____
Total Hours	168

Unlike Spending Plans, Time Plans have the same starting point for everyone: 168 hours. But just as with Spending Plans, the first time you go through it, it doesn't come out quite right. Don't worry.

I've worked with workaholics who went through the whole exercise as earnestly as they could, planning to spend according to their needs and desires in each area of their lives. Then, when they get to the work category, they just put in something close to the same amount of hours they were already working. Needless to say, the hours added up to more than 168; more like 200 hours. Just go back and rework the plan with balance in mind, and your needs as the guiding sensibility. Don't cut out whole categories to make the plan work. The idea is to reduce several categories by a little rather than slashing entire areas. Always look to reduce work hours instead of other hours.

When I met Lynn, her time was spent something like this:

Work	70
Travel to/from work	6
Sleep	45
Television	18
Telephone (non-work)	15
Eating away from her desk	6
Movies	2
Shopping, laundry, seeing friends, dating, family . . . you name it	6
Total Hours	168

Lynn could not figure out how to make even one hour for herself. Even though she could easily identify a whole range of things she would like to do, she could never seem to muster enough energy to do them. When she was finished working, she didn't have the strength or the attention to do anything much: veg out and watch TV, maybe. When you work as long and intensely as Lynn has, the energy you might once have had for other things is eventually stolen. The work forecloses the desire even to remember.

Once we began working together, Lynn came up with this plan:

Total Hours in the Week	168
Self-Care	
Dinner with friends	4
Theater and concerts	2
Therapy	2
Reading	5
Phone with friends	7
Television	7
Art classes	2
Lunch not at desk	3
Pilates classes	2
Day spa/massage	1
Sleeping	49
Eating	6
Walking in the park	2
Church on Sunday	2
Shopping	4
Housekeeping	2
Errands	3
Travel/getting around	5
Family	
Visiting brother	2
Talking to mother	3
Other values	
AIDS organization	2
Buffer (time not planned for)	4
Time to do nothing (important)	4
Total Hours Available to Work	45
Work	45
Total Hours	168

Much better. I know what you're thinking. No, Lynn didn't follow the plan exactly, and she definitely didn't go straight from working seventy hours a week to working forty-five hours a week. It was hard for her. But she was committed to breaking her cycle. So she gave herself the goal of getting closer and closer each month to the Time Plan she made. Again, like the Spending Plan, the Time Plan is what we mean to do. Making that intention into a practical reality takes time and it takes practice. Like the Spending Plan, the Time Plan serves as "true north": it is the direction that is important, not how long it takes to get there. We don't get it right all at once; we're looking for progress, not perfection.

Coming off a workaholic cycle can feel like giving up drugs. You feel empty without your fix. You can feel as if you don't have any purpose in the world, that you won't feel any better doing all that other stuff. Don't believe it. That is your workaholic self trying to convince you to keep the status quo. I know it's hard, but the best suggestion I know of in these times is in the saying: This, too, shall pass.

Wholeness and Continuity

The cunning subconscious nature of a money disorder doesn't go away. After the initial crisis period is over, and once things begin to stabilize a little, you finally breathe a sigh of relief. That is when the temptation sets in to ease up on or even abandon the tools that really work. "Now that I'm out of the woods, does it really matter if I write stuff down to the penny anymore?" or "Why can't I use a credit card as long as I don't run up a bill?" As with any addiction, the road leading to relapse is taken one step at a time. Money disorders require continued vigilance, especially when things are starting to get really good.

The metamorphosis has only just begun. The end of the crisis and the beginning of stability are only the first steps down the path toward a life worth living. A life where your values, talents, desires, and dreams are integrated into everyday living.

Before we go much further, let's make sure that the initial part of recovery is well under way; that a Spending Plan is established and on track, all repayment plans have been established and are in effect, incurring new debt has stopped and credit card accounts have been closed, accurate records are being kept, and a commitment is in place to stop all self-destructive acting out with work and money. Then we can look at how to keep things on track, and how to continue the growth and expansion that the Spending Plan is designed to foster in the first place.

It is important to remember, at any point in the proceedings, that if any of the basics begin to slide, you must go right back to the beginning and make sure to get them back on track before going any further. It sometimes feels like none of the basics apply, once we make progress. The exact opposite is true. Making sure the basics are in place becomes more and more important as we go along.

The idea is to keep both oars rowing in the same direction. A trusted friend or adviser can see when one of our oars has slipped, even when we can't see it ourselves for quite some time. All of a sudden the self-care categories slip into a "less important to concentrate on" mode. Uh-oh. An irresistible urge rises up to pay debt with money that should be going into savings to build a comfortable reserve. Careful. Over time we learn to monitor urges and feelings and to superimpose our newfound judgment upon them, always referring back to the realities of the Spending Plan. It is helpful to have someone you trust, and who understands your situation, to bounce things off. Just make sure he or she understands the whole syndrome.

It has often been said that to recover from an addiction requires a serious reduction of ego. And that is more true than not. It is well to remember, however, that ego reduction has as its by-product a proportional increase in self-esteem. And vice versa. In dealing with a money disorder, it is the *fragile and vulnerable* part of self that needs support and nourishment. Underearners and anorectics present this need clearly. Compulsive spenders and debtors have the same need: they simply must concentrate more on ego reduction and humility to meet that need. When faced with arrogance and entitlement, it is helpful to remember that those are characteristics of how small someone feels inside—not how big.

When you forget to take things one day at a time, another temptation is to get carried away with thoughts of the future. "As soon as I . . ." or "Once I save $ X" or "Once I pay off my creditors" or "Once the kids are . . ." or "When I retire." These are signals that you've moved away from living in the moment. The idea is to live solidly in today. Handling today's challenges is never all that overwhelming, but handling tomorrow's always is. We do our best today to live within a Spending Plan that takes care of us today, and allows us to meet our responsibilities to others today.

Some random suggestions:

> Spend for self-care, not to impress
> Shop for specific needs, not to bind anxiety
> Comparison-shop, get value for money
> Choose gifts for their unique expression, rather than their cost
> Save separately for vacations, computers, etc., then buy them with cash
> Buy yourself a gift
> Take time for reflection; spend time alone
> Leave a comfortable amount of time for each task you undertake

A tool I like a lot is the making of gratitude and wish lists. Make up a list of all the things you are grateful for. Do it often. Then make a list of things you hope will come true. This is a vision of how your life would look if it were going exactly as you wished. Revisit it often. I know there can be a cynical urge to dismiss a tool like this. But trust me, this one is powerful—extraordinary shifts do take place. List your desires in all areas: emotional, spiritual, and of course, financial. Don't skimp. Almost without exception, dramatic changes take place. I remember asking one man, "What were the results? Did any of it come to pass?" His answer was, "Well, yes, an incredibly large percentage of it did. But what really blows me away is how limited I now see my vision was about what to ask for."

I like to use the following exercise to underscore the point: imagine you are at your own funeral, but you still have an observing consciousness. What things would you hope to have accomplished in your life before you get there? Equally important, what do you hope the people in attendance will be saying about you? Write it down.

Are you on that track? The above are the reasons for establishing a supportable financial structure in the first place: so that you can live your life in the most expansive and integral way. So that you can stay, unimpeded by your money disorder, on the track of becoming all that you were truly meant to be.

The Ideal Spending Plan

Another creative way to open up your horizons, and let some fresh air in, is the "Ideal Spending Plan." The object is to look at all the categories in your Spending Plan, and right beside them write down how much each category would be if it were the ideal amounts. I don't mean that you should engage in ridiculous flights of fancy, but how much would it take in each category (and feel free to add categories) for you to feel as if things were just the way you hoped for? You would be surprised how often I see these Ideal Spending Plans have come true over time.

Karen had a Spending Plan that she had been working for a while which looked like this. Next to it is her Ideal Spending Plan.

	Spending Plan	Ideal Plan
Net Monthly Income	$5,974	$13,574
Expenses		
Savings	$300	$1,000

Self-Care		
Opera	$92	$187
Ballet	$92	$187
Theater	$100	$150
Fine restaurants	$300	$645
Yoga	$120	$240
Art classes	$100	$100
Fixed Expenses		
Rent	$1,890	$3,700
Utilities	$145	$250
Phone	$220	$300
Cable	$55	$55
Internet	$20	$70
Cell phone	$60	$100
Home insurance	$75	$150
Health insurance	$391	$391
Car lease	$314	$599
Car expenses—gas, etc.	$100	$150
Car insurance	$95	$150
Car—parking	$0	$450
Variable expenses		
Groceries	$320	$450
Food—coffee shops, etc.	$250	$300
Household supplies	$50	$50
Drugstore—toiletries	$75	$150
Clothes	$175	$750
Movies and videos	$50	$50
Medical, doctors, co-pay, etc.	$30	$30
Professional fees—legal, accounting, etc.	$70	$70
Hair, nails, etc.	$200	$200
Photography	$60	$120
Vacations	$150	$750
Maid	$0	$430

	Spending Plan	Ideal Plan
Beach house	$0	$800
Massages	$0	$400
Miscellaneous	$75	$150
Total Expenses	$5,974	$13,574
Total Net Income	$5,974	$13,574

The whole idea is to give some real thought to the amount of money you believe would take care of you abundantly in every way and then write it down. Looking at it right there in black and white, it is inevitably less than you think. In Karen's case, it's a little more than double. Most people think they would need ten times what they earn for an Ideal Spending Plan, but that is rarely the case.

Once you set down the ideal amount, the notion that it is impossible to attain slips away. Not that Ideal Spending Plans come true simply because you set them down on paper—of course not. I am, however, always surprised at how many eventually do. Karen's did. She got a tremendous new client less than six months after she conceived the Ideal Spending Plan that made it completely possible to spend all those amounts. It took her a very long time indeed until she could feel worthy enough to institute the ideal plan, but eventually she did that, too.

The conceiving of an Ideal Spending Plan is an invaluable exercise. It acknowledges your dreams and desires while accepting that although they they are not today's reality, they may very well be tomorrow's. It also takes fantasy and inchoate desires and recasts them into clearly stated terms.

The realignment of priorities that a Spending Plan provides, is very frequently not enough to displace the ennui of the disillusioned ones, the money obsessed. They need to dislodge the complacency and inertia from the comfortable but passionless and fortified place they occupy. The first and probably the most effective action to break the complacency cycle is to change everything completely. Take a leave of absence. Get involved in a completely different type of project. If you have the means, dive deep into a particular intellectual or creative endeavor. Live in a new culture for a few months. Change everything. If you walk home one way every day, walk the other. If you always make love on Saturday night, do it on Tuesday morning. The idea is to find a path to reconnect you with what mattered to you before the ennui and world-weariness set in.

The Practical Side to Healing Deprivation

Underearners and anorectic spenders need to place a great deal of emphasis on assertiveness, on engaging in life. The deprivation types of money disorders are usually accompanied by a fear of people, or a fear of being found out as a failure and a fraud. Deprivers need to counteract the deprivation-mindedness with proactive steps toward asserting their realistic needs in the competitive world. I suggest taking an inventory of talents and strengths as well as challenges and shortcomings. It is often advisable to get support for this. Curious lapses of awareness and judgment about yourself often cling tenaciously. What is called for here is a realistic view of who you are—not better and not worse.

Deprivers think that by denying their positive qualities they are being truly humble. But unwillingness to see themselves accurately usually comes from hidden perfectionism.

Underearners almost all need a raise. You may say we all think we need a raise, but it is not underearning to be earning less than you want. This is different. Underearners, by definition, are earning less than they are worth. Underearning is the result of shutting down needs and desires in order to guard against competition, longing, and the risk of rejection. The world feels too big and scary. The actual amount of money is not the key. The key is that underearners manage to earn less money than people with similar skills, talents, and experience. Underearning is one of the ways to stay small, to stay deprived.

So asking for a raise is often a good place to start. If you're self-employed, the equivalent would be to raise your rates. It is not necessary that you get a raise, just that you ask for one. Many underearners are literally shocked to find out they *actually can* ask for a raise. They thought you just waited until you got one—or didn't. You don't have to feel that you are worth it yet either (although it's a bonus if you can); you simply have to take the action. In fact, for the underearner and anorectic in particular, the plan to "*act* as if" until you "*feel* as if" is often the only method available. Suffice it to say you do deserve it. In my experience, if you are anything like the underearners I have known, you simply do. That doesn't mean your boss or clients will automatically agree. After all, they have come to know you living in that shell. They may be shocked when you emerge from it for the first time. So might you. Give it time. All you need to do is take the action. Leave the results up to the universe for now.

If you aren't making much money at all, or at least are nowhere near establishing a livable, let alone abundant Spending Plan, this next exercise can stir things up a little, get you off the dime. Make a list of all the ways that you can start making money immediately. I'm talking about ways that are available to you right now. So you couldn't list "become a movie star" as a possibility, unless you already are one. These are things you could do tomorrow, if you wanted. "I don't know if there's anything like that for me," some may say; "Nothing that I can do pays anything," say others. None of those voices matter. The exercise is to simply make the list. Whatever comes to mind—write it down. Don't edit yourself; you can do that later. If you think of robbing banks—put it down. You don't have to actually do any of the things on the list, but there may be some you choose to do.

There is usually something on the list that is a legitimate opportunity to earn some money. I remember people who have cleaned apartments, painted houses, organized closets, did other people's errands, took temp work, sold the stuff in their attic, took Christmas jobs at the mall . . . you get the message. I remember one guy who had "work at McDonald's" on his list, as a sort of dare, because he thought it would point out to me the futility of his position and how he would never able to dig his way out of his rut. "Why not do the McDonald's thing?" I asked. "I couldn't even make enough money there to pay ten percent of my bills—are you insane?" he barked at me. I explained that using this method is not designed to solve things overnight. Neither is this whole method of recovery an overnight thing, for that matter. The point is to take action, make a start, so that the world doesn't feel so out of control. The hope is that you might get a little perspective or be in the place to get some inspiration and see where your path may lead. He took the job, basically to prove to me how absurd it was. He stayed a month. After that month he seemed to be shot out of a cannon; all sorts of new ideas and new income possibilities became clear to him. He is currently earning more than he ever has and feels great about his new work. He maintains to this day that the month he spent at McDonald's was perhaps the most important one in his life.

Have a look at your gifts in the clear light of day. An inventory of skills, talent, and experience is a good place to start when you are considering how to raise income. A lot of underearners are working at jobs they hate, or jobs that bear no relation to their training or talents. Often they are too afraid to apply for jobs that are highly competitive; because the risk of rejection feels too great. Maybe they don't want to take a chance on a challenging position because, if they fail, it would feel like proof of their worst fears. Maybe they don't want to take a chance at all. Underearners seldom believe that letting go of control can lead to something good. Maybe, and this is most common of all, somewhere deep down inside, they don't feel worthy of earning an abundant living, or of doing work that feeds and sustains them.

The Concept of "Right Livelihood"

Reexamination of how to earn a living is not restricted to underearners. People in recovery from a money disorder eventually reflect on ℓ

r livelihood, and whether or not it suits them well.
in the crisis period, and through the stabilizing
is spent getting the expense categories right.
... με result is finding the proportion which best takes care of
...ceds and responsibilities, as well as making repayments to creditors.
The next level of growth, and a key spot of interest to underearners,
is how either to bring in more income or to bring the income in from
a source that resonates more to your talents and your desires.

I'm talking about the principle known as Right Livelihood. Once a
Spending Plan is well established, the idea of whether we are in alignment with what Buddhists call Right Livelihood is right there waiting
for us. Right Livelihood does not mean that you give up a lucrative
law practice to become a poet if you would then have no means of
support. It does not mean you give up temping and do nothing but go
to acting auditions if that would mean not being able to pay your bills.
But, maybe it does mean working reasonably toward those things
without disregarding the needs of your Spending Plan—especially if
you are following your heart's desire. And it certainly means reflecting deeply on just what work you are best suited for and expresses
your unique or creative self.

You need an inventory not only of your skills and gifts but of your
desires and dreams, as well. Ask yourself: "If I could choose any way
to earn my living, what would it be?" "If I imagined myself growing
and challenged and fully satisfied in my work five years from now—
what would I be doing?" If your answers are dramatically different
from how things look today, you may want to consider what has to be
done to change course and to move in the direction of integrity. Usually, when someone decides on a career shift, or on opening a new
business, or to begin training for a new profession or craft, he or she
has to marry that intention with the practical realities of how to
bring in enough income to support the Spending Plan during the
transition. Transitions take varying amounts of time, but tend to be
measured in years, rather than weeks or months. Sometimes it seems

that it is too late to make big changes—it's not. If you're forty-five and really wish you had become a teacher, five years from now you'll be fifty and really wishing you had become a teacher. You could have been five years down the road toward that goal if you had started earlier.

Whether you are coming out of deprivation, or you are seeking more satisfying work, the answer may lie in earning money in more than one way. A lot of self-employed people use a sort of crazy-quilt method of patching together various jobs to get them where they want to go.

When you have a "why" to live, just exactly "how" you will do it becomes less urgent. The idea of working at a job that is less than perfectly suited to you, because it leads you to your destination, could not be more different from working at that same job with no destination. Just ask anyone who has made the switch.

A Return to Simplicity

Recently, there has been a lot of talk about "purposeful simplicity" and choosing lifestyles more rooted in nature and community than in competition and envy. I don't mean to suggest that simplicity is for everyone. But some of the concepts might be worth considering.

For instance, someone who is commuting to a job on Wall Street may be considering a switch to a home-based entrepreneurial business. Some of the practical impact that switch would have on his Spending Plan may embody the simplicity ethic. He wouldn't need to spend money commuting, for one thing. He probably wouldn't need the suits and ties and fancy shoes anymore. His attachment to even more expensive icons of success may dissipate over time as well (such as a mansion on the hill, or a yacht, or a plane, or the relentless needing to judge yourself by whether you are beating the pants off the other guy).

Simplicity may be the most efficient way to get from where you are to where you want to be. That is simplicity at its most essential. The guiding principal in simplicity is to weed out the things that are not consistent with the easy transition from where you are to where you want to go. It's about leading a life that is right-sized. That doesn't mean small-sized. It means right-sized for you. Whatever that is. The right size is the one where you are not overextended; but neither are you underused.

"Where Do We Go From Here?"

Many people want to know how to expand the concept of self-care to concentric circles of care in the world. "Once you have taken care of setting yourself straight, what about the world you live in? What about charity, and what about the ancient spiritual principle of tithing?" Up until now, I have not addressed myself to an area that I consider vitally important to living a life filled with integrity: giving. I don't want to lean too heavily on the biblical wisdom that it is better to give than to receive, but giving is at the least an essential component of feeling rooted in your place among your fellows. Giving is a direct way to express your beliefs, hopes, and values. It is the best way I know of to be a catalyst for what you believe is right, and to provide the currency to make things happen for others. I don't believe that tithing (the tradition of apportioning 10 percent of your income to charity) is always the answer. I do believe that if you are earning enough income to take care of your needs as well as your responsibilities, you may want to begin giving. It doesn't have to be 10 percent. Ten percent is a good guideline; but use 1, 2, or 5 percent until 10 percent fits comfortably in your Spending Plan.

I personally don't believe that the percentage of income is the key feature in a vital giving plan. I believe the most essential part is how it fits into an overall plan for taking care of yourself, and, in this case, for expressing your care for the world around you. Giving a higher percentage, without giving careful thought to whether it expresses your values and beliefs, is not as valuable to my way of thinking as a smaller percentage of income given in a more integral way. When the means and the desire have indicated it, I have helped in developing a philanthropic Spending Plan. Spending must always be in the service of taking care of and expressing ourselves as fully as possible.

A Case Study in Continuity: One Man's Journey

Mark came to see me with his wife, Linda, about three years ago. She was as angry as she could be about the amount of debt they had incurred. Their communication had degenerated into escalating fights and scathing accusations. Linda accused Mark of being a lousy husband who could never be depended on to earn enough money, but could always be depended on to spend tons of money on "boy toys" such as new stereos and computers, cigars and DVDs. He said she had her head in the stars, and that her dreams of a house in Scarsdale were laughable.

In addition to the marital discord, Mark had very real problems of his own to work on. He admitted that he couldn't control himself when it came to buying all the cool new stuff. He also admitted that his work history was more than a little erratic. He never made as much money as he had expected to, and although he was an accountant, he never liked any of his accounting jobs and was eventually fired from most of them. Once fired, he would fall into an emotional tailspin and couldn't find the wherewithal to get a new job until his finances lay in shambles. During these periods he was always too scared to tell Linda how bad things had gotten, so she would go ballistic when she inevitably found out.

Mark had one of those jobs he hated when we met. And he was overspending like crazy. Once he had made a commitment not to borrow money anymore and to live according to a Spending Plan, the plan looked like this:

Income
   Salary $44,000 per year
   Net Monthly Income $2,442
Expenses
   Savings $150
Self-Care
   Cooking $40
   Gym/exercise $25
   Camping $38
   Baseball, football $35
   DVDs $34
   Books $22
   Concerts $23
   Tropical fish $30
Fixed Expenses
   Rent $525
   Gas/Electric $40
   Phone $35
   Cable $24
   Internet $10
   Home insurance $11
   Car payments $169
   Car expenses $95
   Car insurance $52
Variable Expenses
   Groceries $175
   Food—restaurants $145
   Household supplies $35
   Drugstore—toiletries $45
   Clothes $65

Movies and videos	$30
Medical, doctors, co-pay	$10
Haircuts	$19
Vacations	$43
Gifts	$48
Stationery	$8
Miscellaneous	$25
Total Expenses	$2,006
Total Income	$2,442
Balance Available to Pay Debt	$436

Mark never did stick with this plan very well. And he lost his job shortly after establishing it. He certainly never made a debt repayment plan with his creditors. And things were pretty tense at home with Linda.

But after losing his job this time, he did something different. He didn't go into his cave, as usual. He decided to find a job that he liked—regardless of what it paid. So he made a list of all the jobs he would really enjoy having. "Working with boats" was at the top of the list. He had loved boats since he was a kid and had once sold pleasure boats during summer break at college. After doing research, and going on several interviews, he was offered a sales job for a large pleasure-boat manufacturer. The only catch was that the salary was far less than that of his last job; most of the earnings were expected to come from commissions.

When we discussed the options, I asked Mark if he was willing to live according to an Austerity Spending Plan while getting established in this new field. He said he was. And something felt very different about his commitment this time. Mark's Austerity Plan with the new job looked like this:

Income

Salary	$25,000 per year
Net Monthly Income	$1,651

Expenses	
Savings	$100
Self-Care	
Cooking	$30
Gym/exercise	$15
Camping	$24
Baseball, football	$20
DVDs	$17
Books	$11
Concerts	$12
Tropical fish	$15
Fixed Expenses	
Rent	$525
Electric	$40
Phone	$30
Cable	$24
Internet	$10
Home insurance	$11
Variable Expenses	
Groceries	$140
Food—restaurants	$120
Transportation	$63
Household supplies	$20
Drugstore—toiletries	$35
Clothes	$25
Movies and videos	$20
Medical, doctors, co-pay	$10
Haircuts	$19
Vacations	$25
Gifts	$25
Stationery	$8
Miscellaneous	$15
Total Expenses	$1,409

Total Income	$1,651
Balance Available to Pay Debt	$242
Debt Repayment Plan	$242

Mark felt as if he was on the right track with his new job for the first time in a very long time. He committed himself to his Spending Plan, and he monitored it until he was using it at close to 100 percent of his spending after only three months. During this time he set up a dialogue with all his creditors and made his payments promptly. He opened a savings account—something he hadn't bothered with in he didn't know how long. "It was a pretty great feeling when I put that hundred bucks in there when I got my first paycheck. It was an even better feeling to put another hundred in the next month and the next, and watch it grow." And he really liked his job: he was good at it. Instead of waiting for the other shoe to drop as he always had at his other jobs, he began to imagine doing really great work and advancing. His superiors took note, too.

Mark had the same old complaint, however: he was still in what felt like an underearning situation—especially since he started in the off-season and the commissions had not started rolling in yet. He was afraid to ask for a raise in light of being new at the job. But the bigger problem was that in light of how he felt about himself, he was never able to ask for a raise. The truth was simple: he felt that he didn't deserve it. Nonetheless, with my encouragement he decided to tell his boss he thought he was worth a higher salary, and he laid out the reasons to support it.

Mark got the raise. They liked him so much, in fact, they told him he was the best new employee they had had in a while, and he got the biggest raise of his life: 50 percent. His new salary would be $37,500, plus commission. And it was coming into boat-selling season, when he would earn some real commissions, too.

Mark lived with the Austerity Plan for about eight months, until his income had stabilized. By then, not only had his salary gone up by 50 percent, his commissions were almost equaling his salary.

It was time for a new Spending Plan. Mark was eager to give most of what was now available to his creditors, but after working with a Spending Plan for eight months he knew that realigning a Spending Plan required consideration of all categories. We came up with this new plan:

Income
Salary	$37,500 per year
Net Monthly Income	$2,310
Net Monthly Commissions on Average	$2,200
Total Net Monthly Income	$4,510
Total for Spending Plan Purposes (since commissions	
differ over the year—a conservative average for the year)	$3,500

Expenses
Savings	$250

Self-Care
Cooking	$60
Gym/exercise	$50
Camping	$72
Baseball, football	$35
DVDs	$34
Books	$35
Concerts	$30
Tropical fish	$45
Saving for a cabin in the woods	$200
Saving for a classic Porsche	$200
Renting a cabin in the woods each year	$85
Dock space for his new boat—given to him to use free at his job	$125
Saving for a new computer	$76
Saving for a new DVD player	$29

Fixed Expenses
Rent	$525
Electric	$40
Phone	$30

Cable	$24
Internet	$10
Health insurance	$76
Home insurance	$11
Life insurance	$36
Disability insurance	$59
Variable Expenses	
Groceries	$190
Food—restaurants	$200
Household supplies	$35
Drugstore—toiletries	$50
Clothes	$75
Movies and videos	$40
Medical, doctors, co-pay	$10
Haircuts	$19
Vacations	$50
Gifts	$75
Stationery	$8
Photography	$30
Miscellaneous	$25
Total Expenses	$2,944
Total Income	$3,500
Balance Available to Pay Debt	$556
Debt Repayment Plan	$556

It's now three years later. Mark is the regional manager for his company. He is earning $95,000 a year and is in line for another promotion. He has a company car *and* a company boat. While he has paid back a significant amount of debt and never incurred more, he says none of that occurs to him on a daily basis. He never thinks about the debt anymore. He's thinking about the cabin he has his eye on—he now has enough saved to make the down payment.

Savings, Retirement, and Well-Being

People with money disorders have trouble with balance. Creating a systematic and stable approach to savings that takes care of their needs is no exception. The truth is that obsessions with savings, investments, and retirement are completely natural for people with money disorders, but antithetical to a durable sense of well-being. Most people with a money disorder either don't have very much savings at all—or else something in them kicks into high gear once they have substantial amounts. They begin to crave even more. They become completely obsessed with the idea of holding on to it. Or with the idea that it will somehow be taken away from them. I know of a man who has been chained to his money-making chair for his entire adult life. He has amassed very substantial wealth, probably $50 or $60 million, but his entire attention is still fixed on making more. The astonishing thing is that he doesn't feel safe with how much he has.

The same dynamics can be witnessed at every income and saving level. An obsession simply doesn't pay much attention to whether the numbers are big or small. The obsession can take the form of fixed illusions about "magic numbers." Or monitoring bank balances, investments, or portfolios can be the obsessive focus. Or maybe the extreme effort at control manifests itself an an attempt to plan for every possible contingency ("I haven't incorporated a provision for runaway inflation in my retirement planning"). And, of course, there is the old standby of just making more and more no matter what. Or needing to make more than that guy, then that that guy, and . . . you get the picture.

But savings plans, including saving for retirement, begin with self-care today. And they end with self-care today. Who cares how much you were able to save for retirement, if when you get there you've become a miserable son-of-a-gun because you foreclosed on your life in order to save? The truth is that the only way to save for *anything* is essentially the same. You establish a Spending Plan that elaborately takes care of your needs. The top line on a Spending Plan is always savings. Therefore, savings will grow. A liquid reserve fund will be established. Investments will be made. Expanding financially is a natural by-product of allowing the expansion of the heart and the soul.

The problem comes when instead of saving in accordance with taking care of our needs first, a certain savings goal is substituted for the overarching principle of the Spending Plan. That doesn't work and is a sure way back to the obsessive cycle: a sure way to make money the obsessive focus of life, rather than the facilitator of a life filled with well-being.

Live Life Now

The great national obsession with retirement doesn't help. Living a life you would never want to retire from is a much better strategy than obsessively planning to retire from a life you didn't want to lead to begin with. Besides, which of us is promised we will actually make it there? In any case, the vision of an idyllic retirement full of joy and ease is an illusion. If you sacrifice living a vital and expansive life now in order to retire later, you will not be the person you hoped to be when you get there.

I spoke to a union representative recently who said the most common discussion among the membership was exactly how many days, months, and years it will be until their retirement pension kicks in. He told me the story of one man who everyone teases because of how grumpy he is and who hasn't stopped complaining for twenty years. "You guys just wait, everything will be different when my pension kicks in. You won't hear me complaining." I'm not so sure. Have you ever met anyone who complained for twenty years, then one day just stopped? I don't think so. It doesn't work that way.

A lot of entitlement is expressed through complaining. The idea that you are *entitled* to a life of ease or luxury after some certain point is the problem. Maybe you are, maybe you're not. What difference does it make? If you live according to what takes care of you best, and what expresses your truest nature to the fullest, savings and retirement never seem to be very big worries anymore.

Does that mean you don't save? Does that mean you don't plan? Of course not. You just save the best way you can according to a Spending Plan and leave the results up to the universe.

Human resources departments are also beginning to report that more and more employees are obsessed with their stock portfolio and spend more time checking their computers and trading their stocks than doing their work. I know of a dentist who checks his stock portfolio between each patient. I can assure you that if he hears about the inside track to getting some shares of a hot new stock, keeping his patient appointments will not be his highest priority that day.

Saving and planning for the future and establishing a fund that is there for you to depend on are integral parts of recovering and living with a Spending Plan. But there is a huge difference between taking care of savings according to a Spending Plan, which is designed to express your beliefs, values, dreams, and desires, and becoming obsessed with saving, planning, investing, or retirement.

Savings, investments, retirement planning, and wealth building are all consistent with an expanding vision for the future. The only proviso is that these things be done in the same spirit as the Spending Plan. Again, and again—taking care of your needs is the goal, not winning the game. Self-care is the beginning and end of a savings plan, too, not acquiring a certain amount of money. In other words, we save the best we can, and we plan what to do with that money. We don't conceive of a certain amount of money we have to have, and then obsessively set out to get it.

A supportable financial structure must grow with you and accommodate changes in circumstances. I recommend that savings equaling either three months expenses for salaried workers, or six months for those that are self-employed, be kept in a liquid savings account in cash or cash equivalent. That is the amount of money that you keep around just to feel comfortable. For little emergencies. To end the constant worry about always feeling on the edge. To have a fund of money that you can rely on and that can carry you through any bumps in your income.

Once you have established your liquid reserve (remember, you need cash savings of at least three months of expenses if you are on a salary, and at least six months if self-employed), then savings can be used for all manner of things. Saving for education. Or for a down payment on a house. Savings for retirement. Maybe you want a boat, or a new car, furniture, or artwork? It doesn't matter. What matters is to apportion our savings dollars into categories that take care of us. I recommend that savings and investments in each of these categories be as carefully planned as each expense category was in your Spending Plan: a savings plan should delineate each savings category, with specific amounts allotted to each.

Go back to the Spending Plan. I recommended raising savings until it equals 10 percent of income. Obviously, 10 percent is not the limit. It is a reasonable goal, and a comfortable place for most people once they are back on track. Many, of course, will be able to meet the needs of an abundant Spending Plan and still save considerably more than 10 percent.

I'm certainly not going to give you any investment advice. There are more than enough books and advisers available on that topic. Just about any accountant, tax lawyer, stockbroker, insurance salesperson, or financial planner—you name it—offers that type of advice. You will find no dearth of suggestions. What you will probably find is a complete lack of perspective. You have to develop that on your own before you consult with professionals, so they can do your bidding— not so they can impose their own judgment on your situation. That doesn't work out very well.

I know of a woman, by no means alone, who trusts her investment adviser with all her money. He is a well-respected man, and I am perfectly sure that he has her best interests at heart. But they have never had a discussion that would help him to know what any of her interests are, let alone her best interests. He actually acts as a sort of stand-in parent for her. He chastises her when he thinks she's spending too much. He as much as tells her that she might as well not even call if she wants to make a withdrawal—he doesn't let her. Now, of course, she could insist. The money is hers. But she doesn't insist; she has given over her decision making to this man she has invested with some sort of mythic power to take care of her. They seem to have made a tacit agreement to act out some old co-dependent scenario. By allowing this man to control her money, she gets to say that it is about his expertise in investments. And by that means she disguises the emotional interaction.

When your guiding vision is becoming fully yourself, then managing your savings and investments is simply another group of subcategories under "Savings" on your Spending Plan. And the heat of obsession is gone.

Epilogue: A New Way to See

There is an old Talmudic story about a rabbi named Zusya. He was counseling a man who was trying desperately to live according to the standards he felt the great men of the past embodied. The rabbi told him his view: "When I get to Heaven, God will not ask me, 'Why were you not more like Moses?' Rather, He will ask, 'Why were you not more like Zusya?' " In another story from Talmudic lore, a man complained to his rabbi that he was reaching the limits of his endurance, couldn't handle the stress, and felt he was going to snap. "Why are you running so fast?" the rabbi asked. "I am chasing after my livelihood," the man explained. To which the rabbi made his famous reply: "How do you know your livelihood is out in front of you? Maybe you just need to slow down and let it catch up with you."

Money disorders block the natural flow of energy and vitality. They are designed to dovetail with all the feelings about ourselves that keep us under wraps. You can be under some pretty fancy wraps and still be choked off from authentic self-expression by an active money disorder. Money is not the problem, so money can never be the solution. That is why breaking an addictive money cycle begins with self-care, and ends with self-care. The only difference at any given stage of recovery is in the expanding definition of what constitutes self-care.

The big question I eventually ask everyone in recovery from money disorders is: "If your defenses weren't in place, if you were free to follow all the longings of your soul, what would you be doing?"

What are those defenses about, really? What are the truer desires under the surface desires? What deeper longings get displaced onto money? What does money replace that we are *truly* not getting enough of?

Recovering from money disorders begins with the discipline of establishing and keeping to a Spending Plan, making restitution to creditors, and stopping the self-destructive cycle of addiction. But the overall goal is deeper; it is to redress the underlying spiritual and emotional imbalances—building up a solid enough sense of self to courageously assert our needs, and to become our truest and best selves, while allowing the maximum amount of spirit to infuse us.

The first question a compulsive shopper might ask when the urge to shop comes along is properly "What is the anxiety that I bind with my shopping?" rather than "What can I buy?" Digging deep to deal with underlying causes means coming face-to-face with the difference between residual childhood hurts and the desires of the here and now. And calling them by their real names. Sometimes it is not easy to own those desires. So how do we go about integrating what we have spent our lives defending against?

Tolerating joy is a lot harder for a person with a money disorder than tolerating difficulty. Whatever the difficulty, and no matter how critical the problems become—we're used to them. They are ours, and we know how to live there. Whenever someone complains about how hard the challenges of early recovery are, I tell him, "Just wait until you experience true abundance and joy—now *that* is hard to tolerate."

And that is the challenge—uncovering the blockades we've erected to avoid even allowing, let alone inviting, joy and abundance into our lives. Obviously we are not talking about "talking the talk" here. We are not even talking about merely "walking the walk"—we are talking about reorienting the soul as we walk. Embracing who we are, what gifts are legitimately ours to claim, and who we are truly meant to become.

Accepting and honestly feeling pleasure is not easy for most money addicts. If the needs that compulsive spenders and debtors constantly seek to fulfill were actually being met, the craving wouldn't grow and grow. What are they really looking for? Why can't they let it in, even when it comes in legitimate form? Is that the problem? What is it that work replaces for the workaholic?

While the deeper work begins to take root, the practical changes with money work their own sort of magic—while a stronger sense of self develops, the addictive cycle stays broken. Taking action that defeats the addictive cycle has emotional fallout, however. Hopefully, part of seeing things a new way is directing the focus of those feelings back to their original source and not resorting to the same old defenses.

The process is the goal. Although, of course, we have stated goals along the way, getting there is not what matters. It is the becoming that happens all along the path that is what genuinely counts. Transformations take place.

We move from:

Deprivation to abundance
Defensiveness to insight
Willfulness to acceptance
Resentment to gratitude
Fear to trust

Everything about the system of recovery I have laid out is designed to help effect these essential changes.

Deprivation is a world where some of the colors are missing; allowing abundance to replace deprivation is an all-encompassing challenge. Doing so doesn't necessarily feel as if it is a matter of allowing or not; it feels more like something that requires the services of an alchemist. It is well to remember: deprivation is a condition of the soul, not of the bank balance. Abundance is sometimes the difference between wanting what you get rather than getting what you want. It can also be the difference between allowing yourself what you want and denying that you ever wanted it to begin with.

Fear sometimes feels like it is so deep, that it seems to be happening deep in our cells. How does someone switch away from that? And to trust—to trust in what exactly, and to gain trust how exactly? These are the bigger questions that are answered in the small moments when we are committed to change. Once fear diminishes and trust begins, the horizon goes on forever. Integrating life practices such as quietude and meditation, appreciation of beauty, accessing your sense of awe—all help to quell the sense of fear that always seems to over-arch a money disorder.

Acceptance is a practice that yields unexpected results . . . such as peace of mind, and release from obsession. There is no way to adopt a sturdy Spending Plan if we haven't first accepted large chunks of reality. Continued acceptance, as opposed to running on self-will, is a struggle truly made for the lifelong conflict between ego and humility.

Resentments and envy reign supreme for people with money disorders. Making the jump to gratitude is like just asking—and suddenly you're there, in a parallel universe that was there all along. Practicing gratitude requires making an essential shift in perspective. There are always two views of a situation; which one will you choose? "I have such a long way to go," someone laments. "Yes. But look how far you've come."

Courage. Giving up defenses takes courage. Asking for help rather than doing things the same old way takes courage. Moving into the unknown—even when what is known has been painful—takes courage. The truth is that for those with money disorders, experiencing joy or any powerful emotion takes courage.

Money to facilitate our lives then—not to be the focus of them. When we spend in accordance with our values, desires, and beliefs, the meaning that we searched out in all the wrong places naturally materializes.

Index